MW00577066

THE RISE AND FALL
O F
FRATERNITIES
A T
WILLIAMS COLLEGE

THE RISE AND FALL OF FRATERNITIES AT WILLIAMS COLLEGE

*Clashing Cultures
and the
Transformation
of a
Liberal Arts College*

BY
JOHN W. CHANDLER

Williams College Press
Williamstown, Massachusetts

Williams College Press
Williamstown, MA 01267

Hardcover ISBN: 978-0-915081-07-3

Library of Congress Control Number: 2014934352

To the memory of
John Edward Sawyer (1917-1995)
sine qua non

CONTENTS

THE RISE AND FALL
O F
FRATERNITIES
A T
WILLIAMS COLLEGE

PREFACE

In January 2011, the late Carl Westerdahl, president of the Williamstown Historical Society, invited me to give a talk on the history of fraternities at Williams College. Frederick Rudolph, a noted authority on American higher education whose publications include several volumes devoted to the history of the college, kindly read the manuscript of my talk and generously encouraged me to "let it grow" into a book-length study.

The impetus to do so grew when a surprisingly large audience appeared for the talk. They consisted principally of alumni, many of them students from fifty years and more ago, a time when fraternities had come under siege and then were abolished from the campus where they had been a powerful and defining force for a century and a third. I had joined the Williams faculty in 1955, and I recognized many of those in the audience as having been my students

The discussion that followed the formal address was lively and prolonged. Almost immediately, I was on the receiving end of a copious flow of telephone calls, emails, and letters from those who attended the program and others who had heard about it. Fred Rudolph's advice to let it grow was abundantly reinforced. In the autumn of 2011 and again during reunion weekend in June 2012, the Alumni Relations office at Williams organized panel discussions that included me, along with alumni who had figured prominently in the studies, debates, and reform movements that preceded the end of fraternities. The panel discussions, like the program sponsored by the Williamstown Historical Society, drew overflow audiences.

The formal trustee action to replace fraternities with a new residential system had come in 1962, and the fiftieth anniversary of that decision stimulated further attention and interest in the subject. Joined by Bruce Grinnell '62, a key student leader in the move to abolish fraternities, I have appeared in leadership studies classes to discuss the topic of Sawyer's leadership. I became a go-to source for Williams undergraduates writing papers about fraternities. The widespread interest and my own curiosity led to my resolve to take Fred Rudolph's advice and tell this inspiring and instructive story

The abolition of fraternities in the early 1960s was the beginning of a radical transformation of Williams College, one marked by the reorganization of the residential, dining, and social life of its students; the admission of women; the increase of the enrollment by some 80 percent; the acquisition of significant new financial resources; and a far-reaching reform of the curriculum. The principal architect of that transformation was John E. Sawyer, the college's eleventh president (1961-1973). Without Sawyer's vision, courage, resolve, and strategic brilliance, what had been an evident decline in the quality of the Williams experience might have continued. There was nothing assured or inevitable about the eventual fulfillment of Sawyer's vision. Indeed, the outcome of the struggle that he led, with powerful support from trustees and other key leaders from all the college's constituencies, was problematic for several years.

I became a member of Sawyer's administration in 1965, first as acting provost and then as dean of the faculty. I chaired the committee that was responsible for the overhaul of the curriculum and was a member of the committee that recommended the admission of women. After I left Williams in 1968 to serve as president of Hamilton College, I was invited to join the Williams board, which was deeply involved in the implementation of the many initiatives that Sawyer had advocated. In 1973 I succeeded Sawyer and became the twelfth president (1973-1985).

As I relived those momentous events in the history of Williams, I came to appreciate the advantage that my involvement gave me. I personally knew virtually all of the principal actors in the drama, and have stayed in touch with all those still living. The following chapters tell of events that I believe have a relevance, even a utility, far beyond Williams College.

Introduction
THE CLASH OF CULTURES

The first fraternity was established at Williams College forty years after the college's founding in 1793. Kappa Alpha and the fraternities that followed soon became a major force in shaping and defining the college. For a century and a third, fraternities were widely viewed as the most influential aspect of the student residential experience and thus central to the culture of the college.

From the earliest days, there were disagreements over whether that influence was predominantly positive or negative. When the fraternity era effectively ended in 1962, 94 percent of the members of the three upper classes dined in fraternity houses, and 44 percent of them roomed there. Those numbers suggest how pervasive fraternity life had become—and the magnitude of the transformation that would ensue as a result of presidential initiatives and trustee decisions to end the fraternity era.

Since 1833, a succession of presidents and trustees had acquiesced to the long-term symbiotic relationship between Williams and fraternities, in part because of the great popularity of fraternities but also in recognition that the fraternity experience made some positive contributions to the emotional maturity, intellectual growth, and social lives of students, all of whom were men. The governing authorities appreciated that the college depended upon fraternity corporations to meet expensive student needs that otherwise would have been responsibilities of the college. There was also an important, though tacit, recognition that the college and its fraternities shared a set of values by which fraternities chose their members and the college defined its mission.

Despite the interdependence that in time developed between the college and fraternities, secret Greek-letter societies were viewed from their beginning as antithetical in some measure to the Christian values that Williams vigorously espoused both through its curriculum and by means of required religious exercises. Fraternities introduced a clash of cultures to a college that had been indelibly branded as Christian by the Haystack Prayer Meeting of 1806, when a small group of students initiated the Protestant foreign mission movement. Still, resistance to fraternities did not reach crisis proportions until the post-World War II period, when a new clash of cultures emerged, and fraternities came to be identified as major obstacles to the college's educational mission and its ambitions to a high academic seriousness open to all the talents. By then, the growing diversity of the student body highlighted discrimination by fraternities on the basis of race, religion, and whatever individual characteristics offended the prejudices and sensibilities of fraternity members whose votes determined who was chosen for membership. A large influx of World War II veterans brought to the campus students who were not well acquainted with fraternities, and who questioned the values and policies that governed their selection of new members.

For a period of about fifteen years following World War II, issues related to fraternities occupied a significant amount of the time of trustees and top administrative officers of the college, became the principal topic of articles and editorials in the student newspaper, and were a perpetual source of conflict and distraction among students. Various student initiatives and trustee-mandated studies brought about a succession of fraternity reforms intended to end discriminatory practices and weaken the grip of fraternities on the college's culture. Unintended consequences stemming from those reforms further threatened the viability of fraternities and thus presented major problems to Williams because of its symbiotic linkage to these institutions.

Those developments came to a head during the administration of President John E. Sawyer (1961-1973). Sawyer and his trustees concluded, after extensive study by a special committee, that fraternities had become a liability and were impeding the educational development of Williams. Amid much conflict and controversy, and with the outcome problematic at times, they abolished fraternities and created a new structure of residential and social life that lent far stronger support to the college's educational mission. A large part of this story concerns the vision, struggle, and courage required to accomplish that goal. The central actor in this drama was President Sawyer, but the cast was large, and it included many others—students, faculty, alumni, and trustees—whose leadership was essential to achieving an array of far-reaching changes with many interrelated aspects and dimensions.

PART I.
THE AIMS OF EDUCATION:
MISSIONARIES OR GENTLEMEN?

DELTA KAPPA EPSILON, CA. 1880

Chapter 1.
Fraternities Take Root
1833–1881

The first fraternity arrived at Williams College in 1833 during the administration of Edward Dorr Griffin (1821–1836). The welcome that President Griffin accorded Kappa Alpha was based upon a misunderstanding. Such is the account that has been passed along for well over a century and a half by historians of both Kappa Alpha and Phi Beta Kappa.

Griffin was pleased when a small delegation of students went to Union College, in Schenectady, New York, with the purpose of bringing back a charter for a chapter of Phi Beta Kappa. Phi Beta Kappa had been established at the College of William and Mary in 1776, the first Greek-letter secret society to be founded in North America. After initially attempting to combine literary and social functions, the organization decided that its mission was to recognize scholarly excellence in the liberal arts. The William and Mary chapter conferred upon Union, Yale, Harvard, Dartmouth, and other colleges charter-granting rights within their home states. The Union representatives of Phi Beta Kappa thus explained to the disappointed Williams students that they had no authority to grant charters to colleges outside the state of New York.

Williams had first applied for a Phi Beta Kappa charter in 1797. The waiting line also included the College of New Jersey (now Princeton) and Rhode Island College (now Brown). Because of the intense competition for Phi Beta Kappa charters, Harvard, Yale, and Dartmouth had difficulty determining where the various petitioners stood in the queue. Williams became lost in the shuffle, and both Harvard and Williams apparently forgot about the Williams application. Finally Phi Beta Kappa came to Williams in 1864.

In 1833, presumably as a consoling gesture, the Union students had told their Williams guests that they might take home a charter for the Kappa Alpha Society. Kappa Alpha had been founded in 1825 at Union, the first fraternity at what would become a veritable seedbed for the founding of Greek-letter secret societies. After inspecting the Kappa Alpha key that the students brought back, President Griffin noted that it resembled his Phi Beta Kappa key from Yale and therefore assumed that KA must be similar to PBK. But after briefly attempting to combine convivial with literary activities, KA had decided, unlike PBK, to emphasize social life. The other fraternities that sprouted up at Union followed the KA model. In 1834, less than a year after the arrival of KA, a Sigma Phi charter arrived in Williamstown from Schenectady.

The first fraternity arrived on the Williams campus during the presidency of Edward Dorr Griffin (1821-1836).

His comment: "The Kappa Alpha key resembles my Phi Beta Kappa key."

The operations and rituals of Williams' new organizations were secret. Membership required a nomination and election. Fraternities were almost immediately controversial because of their secrecy. Some students viewed secrecy as inimical to the spirit of Christianity and as undemocratic. That reaction led to the formation of a rival organization in 1834 that was both open in its membership and transparent in its activities. Known variously as the Social Fraternity of Williams College, the Anti-Secret Society, and the Equitable Fraternity, the group flourished for more than a decade and attracted more members than the two secret societies combined. Over time, however, it gradually became more like the secret societies, adopting a Greek name, Delta Upsilon, and requiring that new members be nominated. Thereafter its membership rapidly declined, becoming less numerous than that of the secret societies and the non-affiliates. In 1864, its members voted to disband although later, in 1883, it was reconstituted as a regular fraternity under its old name of Delta Upsilon.

Beta Theta Pi had a similar history. Established at Williams in 1847, it dissolved in 1851 only to reappear in 1914. Other fraternities had short lives on campus; they failed to take root, disappeared, and were never heard from again.

President Mark Hopkins (1836-1872) once remarked, "[Fraternities] put men socially...into an artificial and false position."

By the end of the presidency of Mark Hopkins (1836-1872) there were six secret fraternities. Since the college had a total enrollment of just 119 students, and only slightly more than half of them were fraternity men, six fraternities were plenty. Hopkins's hand-picked presidential successor, Paul Ansel Chadbourne (1872-1881), Williams class of 1848 and a professor of botany and chemistry, undertook few initiatives, hindered by the continuing presence of Hopkins, Chadbourne's poor health, and a national economic downturn. One new national fraternity, Phi Gamma Delta, was established in 1880 but became dormant almost immediately. It was revived in 1913 when a local fraternity, Alpha Zeta Alpha, at Williams since 1903, took over Phi Gamma Delta's national charter and name.

Let's look at why fraternity secrecy troubled some but appealed to other members of the college community. It is especially revealing to do so through the eyes of Albert Hopkins, Mark's younger brother and a Williams faculty member from 1827 to 1869.

Alexander Hyde '34 went to Union College seeking a Phi Beta Kappa charter but returned with a Kappa Alpha charter and key.

In 1841, Albert Hopkins published a two-piece report titled "Revivals of Religion in Williams College." The American Education Society, an organization of the Congregational churches, used its journal to present information that measured the prospects of realizing the audacious missionary dream of the Haystack Prayer Meeting of 1806, when sheltering from a thunderstorm, a small group of Williams students resolved to bring the light of Christianity to "the moral darkness of Asia." This group prayer session was itself the product of a religious revival that permeated the Williams campus at that time. The Haystack vision soon widened to include the goal of converting to Christianity the whole of the non-Christian world, as well as ensuring that the hegemony of the Calvinist Protestant creeds and cultures in the eastern United States would extend to the largely empty western states and territories that beckoned settlers. Toward that end, it was important to have information about the state of religious belief on college campuses, the production of and demand for ordained ministers, the demographic profile of the population of clergy, and the pace of formation of new congregations among the denominations and in the various regions, as well as the number of commissioned missionaries and the amount of financial support for missionary activity.

It is difficult to overstate the importance of the Haystack legacy in defining Williams and the influence of the missionary movement in extending the influence of Protestant Christianity in the United States and abroad. President Mark Hopkins had a triumphal vision of Christianity sweeping the world. He measured the success of the college largely in terms of the percentage of its graduates who became ordained ministers. During the college's first several decades, about a third of Williams graduates became clergymen, and the missionaries in the ranks were regarded as the elite.

The Haystack legacy remained prominent in 1893 when a principal theme of Williams' centennial celebration was the role of the Christian college. When Williams celebrated the one hundred and fiftieth anniversary of the Haystack Prayer Meeting in 1956, President James Phinney Baxter also took the occasion very seriously. The principal speaker at the convocation that marked the anniversary was Secretary of State John Foster Dulles, himself the son of missionaries to China. When the Haystack bicentennial arrived in 2006, there was far less attention to the legacy that it represented and awkward uncertainty about how to observe the occasion.

Two circumstances in particular contributed to the differences between the 1956 and 2006 observances: shifts in the demography of the major Williams constituencies, and changes in academic perceptions of the missionary movement, changes that led to emphasis on its ties with American imperialism and commercialism. It became fashionable to dismiss the missionary movement with the clever quip that the missionaries "went to do good and ended up doing well." There was substance to that perception, as illustrated especially by the role of missionary families in the political and business life of Hawaii. President William McKinley, in 1900, appointed Sanford Dole, a non-graduate alumnus of the class of 1867 and the son of missionaries, as the first territorial governor of Hawaii. His cousin once removed James Dole founded the Hawaiian Pineapple Company, later renamed the Dole Food Company, which became the world's largest fruit and vegetable producer. Indeed, the leadership in the overall commercial and industrial development of Hawaii, including sugar, railways, and shipping, came largely from missionary families.

Recent critiques of the missionary movement have tended to neglect its educational and medical achievements, especially in foreign missions. In addition, many missionaries made valuable scholarly contributions in the form of ethnographic and linguistic studies of the people among whom they worked overseas, while North American missionaries made contributions of comparable importance, especially in the establishment of colleges designed to educate freed slaves and their descendants.

Albert Hopkins was perhaps even more passionate than Mark in proclaiming that Williams' principal mission was to produce Christians. More than Mark, who regarded himself as a surrogate father to his students and was playful and affectionately jovial toward them, the younger Hopkins was concerned with the cultivation of private piety and moral purity among undergraduates. His principal responsibility at Williams was to teach science, but he was perhaps better known and more influential on and off the campus as a revivalist preacher whose personal quest for Christian sanctification was legendary. No one was more alert to subtle and insidious threats to students' spiritual health, and Albert Hopkins sought to fortify them against intellectual and moral influences that might corrupt them. Indeed, he hoped that the college would serve as a "house of correction."

As early as the 1820s, he was troubled that many students had joined the Williamstown Masonic lodge. Masonic secrecy ran contrary to the spirit of openness and candor with which Christians, ideally, professed their faith, confessed their sins and shortcomings, and sought and gave counsel in their relationships with fellow Christians. However, the secret rituals of the

Freemasons appealed to students' desire to be "insiders," as members of select and special groups.

Following an extended trip to Europe in 1834 to purchase equipment for the college's new astronomical observatory, Albert Hopkins, on his return to the college, sensed that "a new element had found its way into the atmosphere of the place." He was right: two secret societies had come to Williams—Kappa Alpha and Sigma Phi. He listened as "little collections " of students debated that new development in "apparently angry conversation." An additional theme entered the conversations with the formation, in rapid response, of the Anti-Secret Society, which disavowed secrecy and opened its doors to all students.

Albert Hopkins regarded the struggle between the secret fraternities and professing (or born-again) Christians as a contest for the soul of Williams. He watched with dismay as the student body splintered into small factions with shifting alliances as they tried to control student elections and dominate the college's two literary societies, the Philologian and the Philotechnian. These had been established in 1795, attracting members with their large libraries and their debating and public speaking competitions, but they existed uneasily alongside the secret fraternities, whose members often were not on speaking terms with those in rival fraternities. Hostility in the early years grew so intense that some carried clubs. There was, Albert Hopkins wrote, "no room to urge the apostolic exhortation, 'let brotherly love continue.'" Fraternity members also tended to distance themselves from the constraining conventions of more fervent Protestants who, in general, eschewed card playing, gambling, use of alcoholic beverages, and profane language, all common to fraternity culture at the time.

The early history of Greek life at Williams illustrated for Mark and Albert Hopkins that fraternities were a divisive and distracting force, and they maintained that view even as they resigned themselves to the continuing presence of a culture that was in tension with what they viewed as the mission of Williams. In an 1845 letter to Amherst College president Herman Humphreys, Mark Hopkins complained that fraternities "create class and factions, and put men socially in regard to each other into an artificial and false position... . The alienation of feeling and want of cordiality thus created are not favorable to a right moral and religious state." On his own campus, however, President Hopkins suffered silently, aware that fraternities were popular even with his trustees. In time, he would also see three of his own sons join Williams fraternities, along with Albert's son Edward.

In Albert Hopkins's view and that of others, the clash of cultures did not begin with the importation of the first two fraternities from Union College, though it then took on a special urgency. Drawing upon information that came partly from Edward Dorr Griffin, a well-known preacher before he became president of Williams in 1821, Albert Hopkins described the low ebb of student piety and morals on American college campuses at the time of Williams' founding in 1793. The college's beginning was coincident with the zenith of the French Revolution and the attendant fascination of Americans, particularly the young, with French culture and fashions of thought. Thomas Jefferson for one regarded the French Revolution as a continuation and extension of the American Revolution. One of the goals of what Hopkins called this "infidel philosophy" was to break the authority of the Roman Catholic Church as the established church of France. Rejection of orthodox Christian belief, a "prevailing skepticism, and general laxness of morals" were particularly pronounced at Williams and on other college campuses.

Long after the era of the Hopkins brothers, there persisted the historical memory of how the French Revolution had shaped the early history of Williams. In a book published in 1927, Elon Galusha Salisbury stated: "The college had come into being, as President Griffin used to declare and President Hopkins loved to reiterate, at the commencement of an historical era, when the smoke and ashes of the French Revolution had darkened the skies, and when the shock of the moral earthquake had been felt among the nations of the earth... . It was at a time when gross infidelity...was coming into prominence and exerting a baneful influence over American educational institutions."

During that era, the more worldly Williams students openly ridiculed peers who professed Christian belief and adhered to traditional standards of Christian conduct. As a beleaguered minority, Christian students found comfort and courage in prayer meetings held in student rooms and, eventually, many who had seen it as the wave of the future became disillusioned with the bloody excesses of the French Revolution. That shift in attitudes permitted Christians to reassert their beliefs and lifestyles.

The quiet prayer meetings sometimes sparked revivals that attracted larger numbers of students and spread into the town of Williamstown. The revival meetings at Williams and in the surrounding region in the early nineteenth century were part of a widespread movement in the United States during the period of approximately 1790-1850 known as the Second Great Awakening. As they preached to the migrants who were moving westward through western New York and into Ohio and Indiana and beyond, frontier evangelists appealed to their listeners' emotions, seeking to turn them away from the secularizing rationalism and skepticism that were the intellectual weaponry in the colonial revolt against Great Britain and the forging of a new constitutional order as the independent United States of America was created. The Second Great Awakening was similar to and modeled upon the Great Awakening that had swept through the British colonies of North America in the middle of the eighteenth century and featured the revivalist preaching of such figures as John Wesley, George Whitefield, and Jonathan Edwards. The goal of both movements was to lead people to make public professions of Christian faith marked by confession, repentance for sinful deeds and attitudes, and by a resolve to lead a radically different life. Being a Christian was more than a matter of growing up in a Christian family surrounded by the influence of the church, but entailed a spiritual rebirth, a radical conversion. For a period, Williams, Union, and Hamilton were prominent among frontier colleges, and it is not surprising that revivalist evangelical Protestantism was an important force in shaping them. Yet many students, separated from their families and childhood friends, also felt the tug of fraternities, which fostered friendship and intimacy.

The Second Great Awakening had largely spent its energy by the beginning of the American Civil War. By then, the culture clash at Williams was undergoing transformation as the college became less an extension of the church and more an adjunct of the secular world of business and commerce. Many new fortunes were created as the economy in New England and the northeast region experienced great growth in manufacturing and became less dependent upon agriculture.

Abundant waterpower facilitated the development of mill towns and villages that turned out textiles, paper, shoes, and the machinery used in manufacturing such goods. Banks supplied the capital to finance those industries. Lawyers drew up the legal instruments to create corporations that displaced the small shops where artisans and craftsmen had prevailed. Large merchandising enterprises were required to sell the output of the mills. Canals and railroads, in turn, facilitated the movement of these goods to consumers.

The economic changes accompanied social shifts at the college, as increasing numbers of young men from newly prosperous backgrounds came to Williams, and many would return to those businesses. Nathaniel Hawthorne's August 1838 description in his diary of Williams students as "half-bumpkin, half-scholar" farm boys in coarse broadcloth suits came to seem very much out of date. Williams was becoming a college for gentlemen. Ideally, they would be Christian gentlemen, but fewer became ministers and missionaries. Graduates increasingly entered such fields as science, law, business, and medicine.

The membership of the board of trustees underwent parallel changes as men from secular professional backgrounds came to dominate the board in both numbers and influence, and the role of ministers in the governance of the college steadily declined. The Hopkins brothers and the faculty in general continued to affirm that Williams was a Christian college, but the brand of Christianity that came to prevail was more genteel and less likely to be convulsed by religious fervor. It had far fewer quarrels with the ways of the world, particularly the world that valued economic, professional, and social success and standing.

Mark Hopkins became an evangelist of the new Christian spirit. He gained the approval of the leaders of the rising entrepreneurial class by ascribing their financial success to the noblest of moral qualities, such as hard work, honesty, frugality, and sobriety. That he favored trade protections helped Hopkins endear himself to many who made fortunes from manufacturing and merchandising enterprises and favored tariffs to insulate them from foreign competition. Despite his longstanding unease with fraternities, Hopkins developed, especially in the latter part of his administration, an appreciation for a more comfortable accommodation between the cultures that were earlier locked in intense conflict. Every senior was required to take Hopkins's moral philosophy course, and almost all remembered it for the rest of their lives, whether they were fraternity stalwarts headed for a secular career or non-affiliates bound for mission fields. Under Mark Hopkins's influence and leadership, Williams became, in his words, a "safe" college with an environment to which any and all parents, including both the socioeconomically successful and the upwardly aspiring, could entrust their sons.

Yet even as Hopkins's views evolved toward a merger of church and commerce, they came into tension with the opinions of others within the larger Williams community who had a different understanding of civic, social, and religious responsibility, especially as the Industrial Revolution intensified inequalities among Americans. Professor of history and political economy Arthur Latham Perry of the class of 1852 was arguably the nation's foremost advocate of free trade, which he regarded as in the interest of poor people, especially farmers. Washington Gladden of the class of 1859, a pioneer in the Social Gospel movement, placed less emphasis on private piety and radical conversion, instead calling for the alignment of economic and political institutions and social policies with such biblical injunctions as the Golden Rule. He defended labor unions as essential to the achievement of economic justice.

While Mark Hopkins's trepidations about fraternities seemed to soften, his faculty colleague and critic, John Bascom, professor of English, political economy, and sociology, called for their abolition *and* for the admission of women. Using as his biblical text Matthew 5:15 ("Let your light so shine before men, that they may see your good works and glorify your father which is in heaven"), Bascom preached a powerful sermon against fraternities to the students and faculty on September 6, 1868. He warned of their threat to "true freedom, individuality, and integrity of action." Fraternities destroyed "independence in opinion," Bascom preached, "as a member's mind was "made up for him on every college question." He objected to secret societies

> with no dogmatic assertion that their results are only and necessarily evil; but because they give unfavorable conditions to individual culture, tending, with a decided balance of influence to frivolous distinctions, actions and feelings; and sometimes at least...to expose the unwary to the needless temptation of intimate and pernicious associations. ... We might farther object to secret societies, as creating artificial, vexatious, and often times unjust distinctions and barriers in a community otherwise homogeneous and democratic, and thus limiting that free, social action, those unrestricted opportunities, which are the rights and necessary conditions of social growth.

As they evolved in the latter years of Mark Hopkins's administration and beyond, fraternities existed amid these intellectual and emotional cross currents. There is no evidence that fraternity men were moved by Bascom's appeal; nor was their Christianity typically either revivalist or activist in matters of social justice. It was, rather, illustrated by such good works as founding neighborhood boys' clubs for the youth of Williamstown.

The Young Men's Christian Association (YMCA) movement originated in London in 1844. Its stated purpose was to promote, especially among young men moving from villages and the countryside into large cities, a brand of Christian belief and practice designed to produce a healthy "body, mind and spirit." After spreading to the United States in the early 1850s, the YMCA movement quickly took root on college campuses, where it became the dominant model for student-run religious organizations.

Earlier, Samuel J. Mills, the most influential of the five student participants in the Haystack Prayer Meeting in 1806, had his own secret society (called the Brethren) that developed the plan for the foreign missions movement. As that dream came to fruition, it was not surprising that Mills's name was attached to a succession of Williams student organizations whose purpose was to promote missions and study theology. Then, in 1873, after Mark Hopkins left office, the Mills Theological Society reconstituted itself as the Mills Young Men's Christian Association. Its weekly meetings attracted upwards of three hundred and included faculty, alumni, and students. Its constitution expressly stated that its purpose was to organize the efforts of students, faculty, and alumni "in serving the religious needs of the college and vicinity."

As the definition of religious needs broadened to encompass the health of the body, mind, and spirit as advocated by the YMCA, fraternity men and non-affiliates felt increasingly comfortable in working together. Williams' branch of the YMCA enjoyed such success that it was emboldened to raise funds for a building to house its activities and facilitate the administration of its programs. Jesup Hall (1899), paid for by Morris Jesup, was Williams' first student center, intended to promote, as Jesup said, "all that is good in college life." In the new facility, students—whether or not they were fraternity members—could play billiards, perform plays and concerts, and sponsor lectures. The building provided office space for student organizations and publications, including the Williams Christian Association, whose officers lived there in a suite of rooms popularly known as "the Vatican."

The shift in the religious ethos at Williams was driven by the change in the socioeconomic composition of the student body, as the scions of wealthy and culturally sophisticated families gradually displaced the sons of Berkshire farmers. Fraternity houses became more imposing and took on the functions of feeding and housing their members. In short, fraternities became powerful purveyors of the values and lifestyles of the families who were most attracted to Williams.

Emblematic of the changing student clientele was Frederick Ferris Thompson of the class of 1856, whose unprecedented philanthropy would eventually have a transforming effect on Williams.

Thompson came from a wealthy New York banking family and arrived at Williams intent upon founding a chapter of Delta Psi (St. Anthony) fraternity. Having achieved that purpose, he left after only two years at the college (the "best years of my life," he later said) to join the family business. In 1857, he married Mary Clark, the daughter of a New York governor, and went on to found two banks, which became components of today's corporate giants Citibank and JPMorgan Chase. As a trustee (and the most generous Williams donor of the nineteenth century by far), he had his ear to the ground constantly as he interpreted and responded to the college's needs. Popular with students, he was especially attentive to what provisions would accrue to their educational benefit. These provisions reflected his era; they were overwhelmingly secular, suitable to gentlemen, and free of the fervent religiosity of revivalism.

After his death, in 1899, his widow created a monument to Thompson. She gave the money to build the Gothic chapel that graces the Williams campus as a memorial to her husband. Although it would become the scene of many powerful sermons by such figures as Washington Gladden, Henry van Dyke, Martin Luther King Jr., and Reinhold Niebuhr, Thompson Memorial Chapel seemed an unlikely setting for revivalist sermons or prayer meetings. It was difficult to envision the chapel, so reminiscent of an Anglican cathedral, as a site where wayward sinners might profess a newfound and transforming faith. The chapel bespoke the wealth and taste that also characterized St. Anthony Hall (1886), the Delta Psi fraternity house, which Thompson paid for and commissioned Stanford White, perhaps the most acclaimed residential architect of his era, to design.

In an era of thrusting ambitions, unprecedented opportunities, and vast new fortunes, Mark Hopkins was in great popular demand as a lecturer. He had access to many captains of industry and commerce who were eager to hear him extol the virtues of capitalism and capitalists and the sanctity of private property. For all his accomplishments as teacher and educational innovator, Hopkins did lack certain attributes needed in his presidential role: above all, he was a poor fundraiser. Indeed, he let his trustees know that he did not regard it as part of his job description. He seemed oblivious to the new opportunities afforded him to raise the money that might bring Williams abreast of its competitors. By contrast, President Eliphalet Nott of Union College was especially alert to these trends during his astonishingly successful sixty-two-year tenure in Schenectady (1804-1866). As a result, Union grew vastly richer than Williams. And it took little time for upstart Amherst, founded in 1821, to surpass Williams in wealth and enrollments. When Hopkins stepped down in 1872, Amherst remained substantially ahead of Williams in those comparisons. Its endowment of more than 600,000 dollars was more than double that of Williams, as was its enrollment, with 268 students compared with the Williams enrollment of 119.

Still, Williams was attracting increasing numbers of students from professional and wealthy families. The college extended its reach westward to Illinois, Indiana, Ohio, and Pennsylvania, as well south into the Hudson Valley region and New York City; the latter would soon become a greater source of philanthropic support than Massachusetts. Students came from such distant places as the Sandwich Islands (Hawaii), China, India, and Persia, some of them the sons of missionaries, and occasional foreign nationals, thus giving the student body an international flavor unusual for that era. Moreover, Williamstown itself had become an important summer resort in the 1840s, a development that helped attract students and money. The image of Williams evolved, as it came to be known as a rich college with rich students. Fraternities played a key role in shaping that reputation.

Chapter 2.
The Golden Age of Fraternities
1881-1934

The golden age of fraternities at Williams began with the administration of Franklin Carter in 1881 and lasted until near the end of the administration of Harry Garfield. By the end of Carter's presidency, in 1901, the college's enrollment was triple what it had been at Mark Hopkins's departure in 1872. The number of fraternities had grown from six to ten, with the addition of Phi Delta Theta (1886) and Theta Delta Chi (1891 and the revival of Delta Upsilon (1883) and Zeta Psi (1881).

The average fraternity membership had increased to a more robust twenty by the time Carter stepped down. Including two additional defunct fraternities that were revived (Beta Theta Pi, in 1914, and Phi Gamma Delta, in 1913). Five additional fraternities would appear by the end of Garfield's presidency, making a total of fifteen. That number would remain constant until the abolition of fraternities during the Sawyer administration.

Although in time it would occupy a larger and more imposing house, Sigma Phi in 1857 had constructed the first fraternity house at Williams—and in the nation—that was expressly designed to house its members and serve as a social center. This development pointed the way to a future when fraternity houses would provide dining and social quarters for all their members, and housing for most of them. In the decades to come that became the norm, the very definition of a fraternity house. Combining living, dining, and social life in a gracious and attractive central facility made it easier for fraternity members to bond into a brotherhood. Alumni made fraternity houses their homes when they returned for reunions and visits. Brothers from other colleges knew that a cordial welcome and a room awaited them on any campus where their fraternity was represented.

During the administration of President Franklin Carter (1881-1901), the academic quality and reputation of Williams advanced significantly. The college's financial condition also greatly improved—and Greek life flourished.

Local living arrangements and the network of campus chapter houses facilitated the efforts of fraternity officers and members of the alumni corporations to imbue students with a set of values, standards, and expectations. Representatives of the charter-granting national fraternity bodies regularly made the rounds of local houses to remind them of their charter obligations, bring them news of developments in other chapters, and propagate the distinctive values and culture that marked their brotherhood. Fraternity membership was cherished, and it was the responsibility of every member to attract worthy prospective members. One's fraternity pin was a badge of honor, and for a member to embarrass or dishonor his fraternity was a serious offense.

During the Harry Garfield administration (1908-1934), fraternities came to dominate the social life of the college as never before. In the first few years of the twentieth century, before Garfield's arrival, classes sponsored elaborate dinners and dances organized by class officers and committees. Lasell Gymnasium (1886) was a popular venue for the dances, and photographs attest to the elaborate decoration of that structure in preparation for those festive events. The dancing sometimes lasted through the

37

night, topped off by breakfast. Some dinners and dances took place in regional hotels, not only the Greylock and the Idlewild in Williamstown, but others in North Adams, Troy, and Saratoga Springs.

No Williams president worked harder than Harry Augustus Garfield (1908-1934) to bridge the divide between fraternity men and independents.

During his administration, fraternities reached the zenith of their popularity, influence, and opulence.

With the growing ascendancy of fraternities, however, weekend house parties superseded dinner dances as the principal social events, attracting to the all-male Williams campus hundreds of young women, most of them from women's colleges such as Smith, Mount Holyoke, Vassar, Wellesley, and Skidmore. Some of these parties started as early as Thursday, and some extended into Tuesday. Especially before World War I, those events were heavily chaperoned, primarily by faculty wives. As the enrollment grew and additional campus buildings suitable to large social events became available, a pattern emerged of three big house party weekends a year, one each in the fall, winter, and spring. That pattern did not, however, preclude fraternities, acting individually, from sponsoring additional large social weekends.

Fraternity parties were grand and costly events, with elaborate meals and bountiful drinks, big-name dance bands, tuxedos, flowers, and favors for the guests. Shortly after the beginning of the college year in 1931, President Garfield urged, and fraternity officers agreed, that, in view of the severe decline of the economy, fall house parties would be cancelled. That show of economic restraint, however, did not establish a long-lasting pattern. Coverage of fraternity house parties by student publications suggested that those events were hardly less lavish during the depression years than in the Roaring Twenties. The nation was still struggling with the effects of the Great Depression in 1937, but the attention paid to the spring house parties that year by the *New York Times* provided no hint of hard times. The *Times* story carried the names of all 460 house party dates and reported that the largest delegation ("more than eighty") came from Smith College.

With Saturday classes cancelled on house-party weekends, faculty members often held their own parties, where a favorite parlor game was to rank the fraternities in terms of which women's colleges were most heavily represented on the list of house party dates carried by the *Williams Record*.

Whether entertaining house party dates or faculty and staff members and their families, fraternity men were gracious and attentive hosts. For them, this was an apprenticeship for the post-college worlds of work and social relations. Such experience amounted to preparation for entertaining with the same grace and style in the homes they would soon establish and in such New York and Washington clubs as the University, the Century, and the Cosmos. They were honing interpersonal skills that would prove valuable later in strengthening and expanding business and social networks and sealing deals.

Mark Hopkins remained a presence on campus when Franklin Carter, class of 1862 and Professor of Latin and French, became president in 1881. Unlike his predecessor Paul Chadbourne, Carter learned how to work around Hopkins. Almost immediately, it was apparent that Carter was going to be a dynamic president and an academic leader of consequence. His twenty-year tenure was a period of remarkable growth and improvement.

His accomplishments included outstanding new faculty appointments that brought curricular specialization to Williams, especially in the sciences and modern languages. The buildings that went up during his administration reflected those educational advances, as well as the tastes and expectations of a more affluent student body. Consider the structures that marked his tenure: the Thompson Biology, Chemistry, and Physics buildings (1893), Hopkins Hall (1897), and Jesup Hall (1899). Morgan Hall (1882), built with money from Edwin D. Morgan, a governor and U.S. senator from New York, was the most luxurious dormitory in the United States and the first building at Williams with indoor plumbing and steam heat. Lasell Gymnasium, constructed in 1886, five years before the invention of basketball, was a state-of-the-art facility.

The Carter era also saw the erection of several splendid fraternity residences designed to house and feed their members, among them Delta Upsilon (1885), St. Anthony Hall (Delta Psi; 1886), Alpha Delta Phi (1895), Sigma Phi (1895), and Delta Kappa Epsilon (1898). In addition to being designed by Stanford White, the lavish St. Anthony Hall included a stained glass window usually attributed to John LaFarge, the most admired stained glass artist of his time. Furnishings of the St. Anthony house included a bronze plaque of Thompson sculpted by Augustus Saint-Gaudens, regarded by many as the greatest American sculptor prior to the twentieth century. The Williams campus gained an opulence in sharp contrast to the simple structures—some of them sturdy but others unsteady—from its first century. The new buildings (not least the fraternity houses) proclaimed that this was a college for gentlemen. Jay Angevine '11, who, decades later, would chair the committee that ushered out fraternities, referred to the fraternity houses of this era as "Taj Mahals."

Among the many innovations that Carter brought to Williams was the annual report of the president. In his 1887 report he disputed the growing claim that Williams had become a rich man's college. He would not be the only Williams president to challenge that assertion but, given the array of new buildings and the backgrounds of the students, it was difficult to argue that the college's new reputation was undeserved.

The opulence underscored that Williams was attracting philanthropic support of a magnitude that greatly exceeded its past record. One of Mark Hopkins's biggest fundraising triumphs had come when Boston merchant and philanthropist Amos Lawrence paid for the construction of a new library. Yet, when Lawrence had initially approached Hopkins and asked if the college needed financial help, Hopkins had said no. When the trustees had authorized the construction of a library for a sum not to exceed twenty-five hundred dollars, Lawrence insisted that wasn't enough and instead gave seven thousand dollars to build Lawrence Hall.

The unparalleled generosity of Frederick Ferris Thompson '56 helped make Williams a rich college, and the fraternity that he founded (and whose house he built, Delta Psi/Saint Anthony) was the preeminent symbol of campus opulence.

A different discussion unfolded when Carter approached Frederick Ferris Thompson about the need for science laboratories. Carter dreamed big and Thompson gave big, a total of 175,000 dollars to build the biology, chemistry, and physics buildings that still serve college needs. After the Lasell family had given fifty thousand dollars for a new gym, Thompson decided that the building needed a clock tower, and he paid for it. He was devoted to Mark Hopkins, and when Carter decided to build an administration building in memory of Hopkins and his brother Albert, Thompson was the largest donor. Thompson also provided general financial support and scholarships, and contributed a lecture and concert endowment that continues even today to enrich the college's cultural life. After his death, his widow, Mary Clark Thompson, provided money not only for Thompson Memorial Chapel but also for an infirmary built in 1911 that later became a dormitory. When fire destroyed the chemistry building, she provided the money to rebuild it.

Henry Hopkins, Mark's son, was sixty-four in 1902 when he became president. His presidency was brief, ending with his own retirement in 1908, but the building boom continued during his tenure, with new Phi Delta Theta (1907) and Zeta Psi (1907) fraternity houses, along with the Thompson Memorial Chapel (1905), Berkshire Hall (now Fitch House; 1905), and the new Clark Hall (1908) for geology. Henry Hopkins, it seems, did not share his father's reluctance to ask for money.

The boom did not let up during the long tenure of Harry Garfield (1908-1934) until the onset of the Great Depression. During Garfield's administration six new fraternity houses were built: Chi Psi in 1909, Beta Theta Pi (1913), Theta Delta Chi (1926), Psi Upsilon (1927), Phi Gamma Delta (1928), and finally Phi Sigma Kappa (1931). Delta Phi came to Williams in 1926 and moved into the Gale Mansion on Ide Road. In 1952, after its original home was destroyed by fire, Delta Phi moved to what is now Agard House, on South Street, which had been constructed in 1906 as the Leake family home and belonged to the Tracy family when Delta Phi acquired it.

While the Garfield years witnessed the zenith of the fraternity movement, the college's prosperity was evident in other buildings built during the same period. Currier Hall (1908) went up just as he took office. The Freshmen Quad, with Williams Hall (1911) and later Sage Hall (1923), was created during the Garfield era. Chapin Hall, initially named Grace Hall (1912), provided the college a magnificent auditorium spacious enough to accommodate large ceremonial events previously held in the First Congregational Church and then at Thompson Memorial Chapel. Stetson Hall, a sturdy and attractive building, was built in 1922 as the college library. Then there was Lehman Hall in 1928, which provided even more luxurious student living quarters than Morgan.

Even as he presided over the most robust period of fraternity development, President Garfield was deeply concerned about the widening gulf between the fraternity haves and the non-fraternity have-nots. The son of a slain president of the United States, Garfield was probably the most widely known Williams president when he assumed the office. A patrician figure who was at home in the inner circles of wealth and political power, he was also a progressive politician with an agenda that closely resembled those of Theodore Roosevelt and of his close friend Woodrow Wilson, under whom he had served as a political science professor at Princeton. His vision of Williams as a training ground for political activists and good citizens was manifested by his founding of the Institute of Politics, a summertime conference that, during the period of 1921-1932, brought political leaders, statesmen, scholars, and press representatives from throughout the world to Williamstown for discussions and lectures on peace, disarmament, and international economic problems in the wake of World War I. Garfield's vision of Williams was compatible with Gladden's Social Gospel message and the slightly later iteration of the Social Gospel advocated by theologian and Baptist pastor Walter Rauschenbusch (1861-1918), who emphasized that Christianity was a political religion more concerned with combating the sins of "suprapersonal entities," such as oppressive governments and exploitive corporations, than the evils committed by individuals. Garfield's vision was clearly distinct from Mark Hopkins's ideal of private piety as the goal of the Williams experience. It can also be seen as a somewhat secularized iteration of the Haystack heritage.

With respect to the role of fraternities at Williams, Garfield's democratic impulses trumped his patrician instincts, as he worked to make the Williams experience and community as inclusive as possible. During Garfield's twenty-six years as president, the demography of the college's student body came to reflect, at various times, the growth of new American populations. The student body included increasing numbers of Catholics, especially those of Italian and Irish heritage. As a rural college at some distance from major urban concentrations of new immigrants, Williams attracted relatively small numbers of students from those groups, but even small infusions of men with diverse cultures and histories set the college apart. Tensions developed between the white Protestant New Englanders for whom Williams was established and the newcomers, as the college grappled with questions about how accommodating and adaptive Williams would be, and the degree of assimilation that could be reasonably expected of the newcomers.

These issues were sharpened by the modest growth of the Jewish student population during Garfield's first decade, beginning in 1908, when some classes had as many as a half dozen Jews. A similar, but even more modest, pattern of growth in the number of black students occurred during the period of approximately 1920-1930, when some classes had as many as three black members.

With such tiny but growing numbers, the question arose whether Jewish and black students would be acceptable as pledges by fraternities. For Garfield, however, the more prominent issue concerned the large numbers of students who, sometimes by choice but usually by deliberate exclusion, did not join fraternities. Indeed, up through the end of Mark Hopkins's administration in 1872, only about half of the students belonged to fraternities.

It was this larger excluded population that Garfield had in mind when, in 1909, soon after taking office, he encouraged the formation of the Commons Club for non-fraternity members. Later renamed the Garfield Club in his honor, the Commons Club provided non-affiliates comfortable and inviting living quarters in new Currier Hall, which included a dining hall and social spaces. Garfield's aim was to offer a residential and social experience on a par with what fraternity members enjoyed. His ruling some fifteen years later that fraternities might pledge no more than 75 percent of the members of a class was meant to ensure a population of candidates for the Commons Club that would be large and diverse enough that the club, in its membership as well as its physical quarters, would more closely resemble fraternities.

In one of a long series of unintended consequences of such reform efforts, Garfield's quota system made fraternity membership more prized than ever and thereby exacerbated rather than ameliorated the problem of exclusivity that Garfield sought to solve.

Another complicating factor was that both the fraternities and the Commons Club refused to admit any members from the very small population of black students. In 1925, as the clash between Garfield's aspirations for the college and its entrenched fraternity culture deepened, the president appointed a committee of six fraternity men and four neutrals to grapple anew with the question, present since Williams' founding, of what might be done to bring unity and cohesion to the student community. In the introduction to its report, the Committee of Ten, as it was known, made it clear that in their judgment there were limits to what the college could do on that front. The report declared, "Our purpose is to assure every man at Williams of equal opportunity in academic, extra-curricular and social activity, in so far as this is compatible with the ability of the men concerned. Yet we know that the result of rushing season makes a vast difference, and the Neutral has not the opportunities of the Fraternity man." The report went on to conclude, in effect, that there were ineradicable differences between the fortunes of fraternity and non-fraternity men because of "obstacles resulting from the natural inferiority of some men."

The primary focus of the Committee of Ten was understandably on the sizeable population of white Protestants who did not receive fraternity bids. But the failure of any black students to gain admission to the Commons Club or the fraternities could only mean that, in the minds of white Williams students, race had much—if not everything—to do with superiority and inferiority. When Clinton Knox of the class of 1930 was denied membership in the Commons Club, he and some other rejected students asked for a meeting with President Garfield to protest their exclusion.

An African American student with a superior academic record, Knox was a graduate of New Bedford High School. He subsequently earned a Ph.D. at Harvard and, following a faculty appointment at Morgan State University, he became a research specialist at the State Department, at that time the principal government agency for gathering intelligence information. Later, Knox joined the Foreign Service, serving in numerous diplomatic posts, including ambassadorships in Honduras, Benin, and Haiti. Presumably the "natural inferiority" that kept Clinton Knox out of the Commons Club was not intellectual ability. The inescapable conclusion is that being black was his disqualifying characteristic. In a 1992 interview, Ferdinand Thun '30 recalled that Knox, his classmate, reported that at the meeting President Garfield had admonished him and the other students: "I think you gentlemen should realize that gentlemen do not go where they are not wanted."

When denied admission to the Commons Club, Clinton Knox '30 was told that "Gentlemen do not go where they are not wanted."

When asked why Garfield would have rebuffed Knox and his friends so sternly, Professor Frederick Rudolph '42 surmised that the challenge from Knox put Garfield in an uncomfortable position. If he had pushed for the admission of black students to the Commons Club, that would have damaged his effort to make the club more inclusive than the fraternities but not so much unlike them (that is, racially integrated) that it might lose its appeal to a broad range of students. Although we do not know President Harry Garfield's personal views on race, it is known that

46

his father, James A. Garfield, was unusual among Reconstructionist Republicans in the degree of his commitment to civil rights. However uncomfortable he may have been in rebuffing Clinton Knox and his friends, Harry Garfield ended up by acquiescing in racial prejudices and stereotypes that were widespread. Notwithstanding this treatment, Clinton Knox was a loyal alumnus throughout his life.

In the first decade of his long presidential tenure, Harry Garfield pursued important changes at the college. He was determined to bring a fresh, vital rigor to the Williams education, an atmosphere of intellectual ferment among faculty and students. He spearheaded a modernization of the curriculum in 1910-1911, creating a model of coherence and structure for baccalaureate higher education. Thus, it is painful to observe the ironies and the unintended consequences, such as the plans for the Commons Club, which undermined his efforts to build an inclusive community embracing the academic, social, and residential aspects of college life.

His insistence that Williams retain a four-year Latin admission requirement, which many colleges and universities had modified, led to a similar result. A teacher of Latin at St. Paul's School in Concord, New Hampshire, early in his career, Garfield viewed Latin as a guarantor of academic seriousness. One of his goals was to make Williams' academic standards more rigorous but, by the end of his tenure, Williams was scrambling frantically to fill the freshman class, largely because of the four-year Latin requirement. The trustees reduced the requirement to two years of Latin or Greek plus three years of modern foreign languages just as Tyler Dennett succeeded Garfield. In the meantime, the college had remained heavily dependent upon the more prestigious prep schools to supply students who could meet the requirement. Since the graduates of those schools generally came from wealthier families, their sons were also better able to afford the more expensive lifestyle of fraternity members. The result was

47

a demographic homogeneity of the student body that both reinforced the image of Williams as a rich man's college and entrenched fraternities all the more deeply in student life.

It is noteworthy that the energy and imagination that marked the early years of Garfield's administration faded after the first decade. When the United States entered World War I in 1917, Garfield yielded to the plea of his friend and colleague Woodrow Wilson, by then president of the United States, to come to Washington to head the Fuel Administration, the agency that controlled the production, distribution, and prices of coal and oil. Thus, Garfield was on leave from Williams from July 1917 to December 1919.

Returning to his desk in Williamstown, Garfield watched Wilson's failed attempt to persuade the American people and the U. S. Senate that it was in the interest of the United States to join the League of Nations. Beginning in 1921, and continuing through 1932, Garfield spent several months a year organizing and administering his Institute of Politics. To many, Garfield in those years seemed more interested in the Institute than Williams. During Garfield's numerous and prolonged absences from the college, the president *pro tem* was Carroll Lewis Maxcy, the vice chairman of the faculty, who lived on Hoxsey Street, inspiring a student ditty, "Maxcy of Hoxsey, prexy by proxy."

By the time Garfield retired in 1934, in the midst of the Great Depression, his had become something of a shadow presidency, his reform hopes long since faded. Ignoring Garfield's efforts to subordinate them to the college's educational mission, fraternities had flourished as never before in the Roaring Twenties, as they flaunted a lifestyle symbolized by raccoon coats, hip flasks, Stutz Bearcat sports cars parked in fraternity house driveways, and membership in New York and Boston Social Registers. Under the shock of the national economic emergency, fraternities had retrenched, cutting expenses and charges, but they remained remarkably successful in blocking "the scholastic traffic," as the *Alumni Review* termed it in October 1932. Thirteen of the fifteen fraternities failed to maintain even "average scholarship," which raised the question of whether Williams

48

College in the Garfield era existed as an educational institution or primarily as home for fraternities and their social functions.

Following an early period of intense engagement with the faculty, Garfield later grew lax with respect to faculty appointments and promotions. His successor, Tyler Dennett, inherited a faculty that included numerous members who were deemed to be unqualified for promotion but who were permitted, nonetheless, to stay on indefinitely, first as untenured assistant professors (some for more than twenty years), and then, by action of the trustees, as tenured associate professors with the provision that they would never become full professors. Dennett was angry and dismayed to discover the situation, and it energized and focused the most significant contributions of his administration.

PART II.
CRISIS AND TRANSFORMATION: SECRET SOCIETIES AND OPEN LEARNING

DELTA UPSILON HOUSE PARTY, CA. 1930

Chapter 3.
Mixed Signals, Missed Opportunities
1934-1937

When Tyler Dennett, class of 1904, was an undergraduate at Williams, approximately half of the college's students belonged to fraternities, a proportion that had varied little since the end of the presidency of Mark Hopkins in 1872. However, when he addressed the students, in fall 1934, during his first semester as president, Dennett noted that fraternity membership had gradually crept up from the 75 percent cap that Garfield had established a decade earlier. Dennett projected a time, not too far distant, when 90 percent of students would be fraternity members. Said he, "It will never get beyond that point. There will always be 10 percent not included in fraternities, and when you get that division, you're going to have 10 percent lost souls on the campus for four years. If it does get to that point—and we're approaching it—I will say to those boys and their parents: 'It would be better to go somewhere else and start over.'"

On the face of it, Dennett's statement might have appeared as the preface to a plan of action to prevent the development of a colony of lost souls, to achieve Garfield's aims in establishing the Commons Club by bringing residential and social inclusivity to the Williams campus. As we have seen, Garfield's plan in fact increased exclusivity in the student body, most clearly along racial and ethnic lines. The impact on black enrollment was especially dire, with no black freshmen enrolled at Williams during the final three years of the Garfield administration (1931-1933). And the college admitted not a single new black student throughout the brief administration of Dennett. Blacks again appeared in entering classes only after World War II, when James Phinney Baxter was president. Amherst College fared only slightly better with regard to black enrollments during that same stretch of years, lending credence to the argument that economic conditions relating to the Great Depression were an important factor, as Dennett had claimed.

It is interesting that in his speech Dennett did not seem to view Commons Club membership as adequate for the salvation of all those who otherwise would be among the so-called lost souls. Even so, Dennett was keenly aware that the scholarly performance of Commons Club members was superior to that of any of the fraternities. Indeed, he expressed strong approval of the Commons Club by becoming a member himself.

Though Tyler Dennett (1934-1937) regarded fraternities as havens for drunken and licentious behavior, he thought them capable of redemption.

Was he, then, building an argument for the elimination of fraternities? Not likely. The conditions that set the stage for such revolutionary action would appear only in the aftermath of World War II. When Dennett took office in 1934, he would have been at least generally aware that his trustees were strongly committed to fraternities. Their staunch support of the fraternity system was voiced in 1936 in the report of a four-member trustee special committee (one of whose members was James Phinney Baxter) on campus social conditions. This trustee committee's charge was, once again, to bring to the board recommendations designed to produce greater campus unity and cohesion.

The report the special committee produced launched immediately into its topic by asking, "Is there any intent in our approach to this problem to abolish or to modify in an important way our present fraternity system?" The answer to that fundamental question could hardly have been more clear and unambiguous. "The answer of the committee to the first question...is most emphatically no. We do not believe that the question merits extended discussion." The committee's one large policy recommendation was that the ratio of fraternity men to independents be moved gradually and after extensive campus discussion to sixty/forty instead of the seventy-five/twenty-five quotas that Garfield had established. While the committee acknowledged that such a change could create significant financial problems for the fraternities, there appeared to be no recognition that reducing the fraternity quota would likely make fraternity membership more prized than ever and thus risk widening rather than narrowing campus divisions. Within a few months after the committee's report went to the board, any impact its recommendations might have had was lost in the aftermath of Dennett's troubles with alumni and trustees that led to his resignation.

Given his various statements and decisions concerning the kind of education Williams should be offering and to whom, it would appear that Dennett was telling the fraternities and the Williams community generally that they must be more inclusive and more diverse, as well as more committed to academic pursuits, but that the achievement of these goals would not require radical discontinuities and disruptions. He clearly believed that fraternities needed redemption, but not that they should be abolished. As an undergraduate, Dennett had been a member of a local fraternity, Alpha Zeta Alpha (later chartered as Phi Gamma Delta), which promoted scholarly accomplishment and welcomed Jewish members. He knew from that experience that fraternities did not have to inculcate and cultivate the undesirable lifestyles and values that he was quick to see they characteristically exhibited at Williams.

Dennett remains a fascinating but puzzling figure. Like Garfield, he came to the Williams presidency from a professorship at Princeton. He was a distinguished diplomatic historian; his biography of John Hay, secretary of state to William McKinley and Theodore Roosevelt, won the 1934 Pulitzer Prize in biography. It is easy to understand why highly respected members of the Williams faculty would have applauded the trustees' decision to appoint him president.

His background was not atypical for a Williams student or president. Born in Wisconsin as the son of a Baptist minister, he grew up in Rhode Island and started his college career at Bates College before transferring to Williams after one year. He earned a degree from Union Theological Seminary after graduating from Williams and, for a brief period, he was a Congregational pastor. Thereafter he worked for Protestant foreign missions organizations and became a scholar of American foreign policy in Asia. That expertise led to a State Department appointment, where he was the highly regarded head of publications. He came to Williams from the Princeton faculty.

Dennett was proud of his New England ancestral heritage. The Williams student periodical *Sketch* carried a biographical portrait by Richard Lovell '41 that represented him as having been molded by the emotional fervor of New England Congregationalism "and the dogged, overpowering persistence of the hard-bitten fighter on the New England frontier." Dennett yearned for a return of what he described as the rugged and resourceful individualism exemplified by colonial New Englanders and admirably modeled by Mark Hopkins.

Dennett deplored the corporatizing of America, as faceless business corporations, law firms, medical clinics, and other organizations replaced the larger-than-life individuals who once defined and dominated national public life. He viewed the welfare programs of Franklin Roosevelt's New Deal as dangerous threats to the spirit of self-reliance that enabled New Englanders to conquer the wilderness and build new lives under harsh challenges. He wanted to see in Williams graduates the traits of character and qualities of mind that would equip them for front-line leadership where they would blaze their own trails and risk failure and defeat. But the conditions that he found at Williams convinced him that the college was not preparing students for such lives.

Indeed, no aspect of Williams failed to evoke his contempt, disgust, and impatience, and he expressed those attitudes with no pretense of tactfulness or subtlety. He called the student body lazy and aimless. He described it as populated by privileged "nice boys" who had gotten where they were by good fortune, not their own efforts. According to Dennett, fraternities promoted a "drunken and licentious" lifestyle, and their "Hell Week" antics were "cow college stuff," mixing cruelty and public displays of bad taste.

The faculty impressed him no more favorably than the students. He saw them as cowards and nullities lacking the courage and capacity to express and defend their views in publications available to their peers in the larger academic community. Only a notable few, including Professor T. C. Smith and Professor James Bissett Pratt, had, Dennett declared, published anything of merit.

Notes left by T. C. Smith reported that as Dennett became acquainted with the Williams curriculum, of which Garfield was the principal architect, he claimed that his predecessor knew nothing about education and that his curriculum was "elaborate nonsense." To his credit, Smith stood up to Dennett. A quarter century before, Smith had played an important role in gaining faculty approval of Garfield's curricular proposals, and he would have an even larger part in helping shape Dennett's general thoughts into precise plans and then gaining their unanimous support from the faculty. He won the respect of Dennett, who named him to the newly created office of Dean of the Faculty. Smith, in turn, admired Dennett's goals for Williams and worked hard for their achievement. Yet, he also saw Dennett as "one of the most isolated persons I ever knew," one who was prone to the "habit of acting alone, completely solitary," and "a very suspicious man, looking for concealed motives and unavowed objectives on the part of all sorts of people."

Unconstrained by tenure rules, Dennett purged the administrative and staff ranks of those he viewed as misfits and incompetents. Carroll Lewis Maxcy, as vice chairman of the faculty, and second only to the president in administrative authority, was spared the guillotine only because he was due to retire at the end of June 1935, at which point Dennett abolished the position of vice chairman. Dennett dismissed the director of admissions, the assistant dean, the head librarian, the treasurer, the chaplain, the college doctor, and the swimming coach. The dismissed assistant dean, Jack Leonard, who was also a Bennington meat dealer, had been responsible for fraternity discipline. A tacit understanding had it that Leonard was not greatly concerned with the behavior of fraternity men as long as they were discreet.

Dennett made clear that he wanted professors with forceful personalities, men who would stake out clear positions, and do it with combative relish in Dennett's own challenging style. He invited faculty and students to behave that way with him, believing that truth emerged from the clash of ideas. An outstanding football player in college, Dennett was known as "Tiger" for his gridiron exploits, a nickname that also fit his manner and style as professor and president. Given the ethos of civility that prevailed at Williams, however, many who agreed with Dennett's educational aims and admired his accomplishments were uncomfortable with his style. Faculty members who stood to gain most from Dennett's desire to base salaries purely on merit took issue with him when he argued that the college should not restore the salary cuts that Garfield made in the early years of the Great Depression, and use the money instead to improve the salaries of those most deserving. They argued that Dennett had a moral obligation to honor Garfield's promise.

Given his style and temperament, it is not surprising that Dennett evoked both admiration and outrage among the various constituencies of Williams. Yet even his strongest critics acknowledged that Dennett's actions as president, especially his personnel decisions, strengthened Williams significantly. He left a lasting positive legacy that provided a foundation for the institutional progress achieved under his successors. He was comfortable with students and reached out especially to student government officers and editors of student publications. (At the same time, students complained that as they crossed paths with the president on campus, he did not bother to greet them.) He strengthened the curriculum that he inherited from Garfield by adding comprehensive examinations and instituting a strong honors program. Under Garfield, department chairs had been little more than clerks, but Dennett appointed a cadre of strong department heads and gave them greatly enlarged responsibility and authority in the appointment, promotion, and evaluation of their department members.

Especially in view of his short tenure and that he was boxed in by the actions of his predecessor and an acquiescent board that insisted upon retaining faculty members who were deemed unworthy of full professorial rank, Dennett appointed a surprisingly large number of outstanding faculty. He was ruthless in denying reappointment to non-tenured faculty members who failed to meet his standards. At the end of his first year in office, twelve faculty members left Williams, just two by retirement. By the end of his three years as president, Dennett had appointed more than a third of the faculty. As a result of his contributions, Williams became a much more academically serious institution, changing the ethos in a way that, over time, students and faculty would begin to question more deeply the role of fraternities at Williams.

When President Dennett surveyed the Williams student culture and demography, he saw socioeconomic homogeneity as a serious liability. The college needed, as he famously remarked in 1936, more than "nice boys." That speech to the Boston alumni portrayed Williams graduates as well-bred, agreeable, and pliable men who typically ended up in established and secure enterprises such as big banks, big law firms, big manufacturing companies, and big hospitals. Too seldom were they trail-blazing leaders standing at the frontiers of their fields. Dennett hoped to shake up the complacent institution nestled in the Berkshire hills.

In an April 1937 speech to New York alumni, Dennett declared that the "perfect condition" for Williams was as a "community in which there would be lacking none of the constituents of the American people." He repeatedly stressed that he wanted a more democratic college, whose students would be drawn from and feel at home with people of all classes and conditions. At the same time, however, he often emphasized in speeches and writings that Williams should be educating fewer, not more students, but doing a far better job at the task. Disputing the assumption that it would be in the national interest to have more college graduates was not likely to win popular support. On the one hand, he wanted Williams to be more democratic in the composition of its student body; on the other, he was attracted by the goal of producing an educated aristocracy, albeit an aristocracy based on merit.

Dennett's campaign to have Williams become more "like the nation itself" was conditioned by the fact that he viewed diversity almost altogether in socioeconomic terms. He wanted more students at Williams from families with modest means. The men the college most needed, he argued, were far more likely to be found in public high schools than private boarding schools. The challenge, he said, was to find them and to keep them when they came to Williams.

The search would be limited by Dennett's strong preference that the missing and underrepresented groups he wanted at Williams would be Christians and, in particular, not Jews. His President's Report for 1935-1936 is revealing on that point. He stated:

> The Sunday morning chapel service has been
> presented to the undergraduates as an essential
> part of the program of a liberal arts college.
> While there was some slight objection to it, it
> appears to have been confined chiefly to
> undergraduates who entered college without the
> background of Christian homes. The complaint
> was of such a character as to underscore the
> necessity in the selection of each incoming class
> of maintaining a large degree of homogeneity in
> the composition of the undergraduate body. It
> should be understood clearly that Williams
> College is a Christian college in which religion is
> regarded as an essential part of culture. Those

who do not share this conviction will not be
completely happy in Williams. Those who are not
willing to acquiesce probably should not be
admitted to the college. If those having such
convictions are actually entered and find the
religious life of the college not to their liking,
they should withdraw.

Given this view, it is not surprising that through the years
it has been widely believed and reported that Dennett banned the
admission of Jewish applicants. However, members of the classes
admitted during his administration (1939, 1940, 1941) have
identified Jewish classmates, and official records from that era
regarding the religious composition of the student body include
modest numbers every year under the category of Hebrew. The
Williams alumni body included such publicly prominent Jews as
New York Governor Herbert Lehman (class of 1899), the first
Jewish fraternity member, and famed civil rights lawyer Morris
Ernst (class of 1909). The college's newest and nicest dormitory
was Lehman Hall (1928). Perhaps Dennett was not prepared to
face the adverse publicity that would surely have resulted from the
curtailment of Jewish enrollments, and hoped instead that his
comments would subtly discourage Jewish applications.

It is clearer that Dennett's ideally diverse student body
excluded African Americans. They should seek educational
opportunities elsewhere, he argued, because of the attitudes of
white students that guaranteed their exclusion from both
fraternities and the Garfield Club. Urban colleges, he suggested,
would offer them a better social experience. In a memorandum of
January 14, 1935 to Professor Harry Agard, who oversaw the
admissions process at the outset of Dennett's administration, the
president laid out the argument. It was not in the interest of
young black men, Dennett wrote, "or to the advantage of the
colored race" for them to attend Williams "under the existing
financial situation."

The coincidence of the disappearance of the black
student presence on the Williams campus with the onset of the
Great Depression was significant, Dennett insisted. And he was

not exaggerating the difficulties created for black students when fraternity jobs that were once available to them now went to needy fraternity members. Still, he seemed oblivious to the resourcefulness of earlier generations of black students in contending with disadvantages and hardships while, in numerous notable cases, excelling academically. Gordon Davis '63 related entertaining accounts from his father, Allison Davis, valedictorian of the class of 1924, and later a renowned social anthropologist at the University of Chicago, of how black students from Williams attended dances sponsored by Pullman car porters during their layover stops in North Adams. The capacity of motivated students to overcome social handicaps should not be underestimated.

Perhaps it would not be fair to condemn Dennett for displaying such views toward black Americans; certainly, such thinking was commonplace among whites in that era. His refusal to press for change in attitudes regarding the admission of blacks was fundamentally no different from the response of Garfield when Clinton Knox and his fellow students pressed for admission to the Commons Club. Furthermore, the failure of Williams to admit any black applicants during the three years of the Dennett administration did not represent a radical break from the record of the Garfield administration during its final three years, when no new black applicants entered.

There is no evidence that Dennett felt any sense of responsibility or made any effort to change student attitudes and provide leadership in creating a more hospitable climate for those with backgrounds different from that of the majority, even though that would likely have served his mission to elevate the college's educational standards. In other respects, Dennett was vigorous to the point of offensiveness in attacking the Williams status quo in pursuit of his reforms. But in the case of racial relations, he was passive, defensive, and tended to cast blame elsewhere, as though he were helpless in the face both of the commonplace bigotries of the times and, closer to home, of racism among Williams fraternity members.

Garfield and Dennett did not differ markedly from the defenders of fraternities in how they viewed the demographic make-up of the Williams student body. The core group consisted of the white Protestants for whose benefit the college was originally established. It was from that core that fraternities chose their members. The core group itself, however, included a large number of young men who were viewed as lacking the socioeconomic cachet necessary to gain fraternity membership. They were the intended beneficiaries of the reforms that Garfield and Dennett promoted. More remote and much smaller fringe groups consisted of Jews and blacks. Their contributions to the college's classroom culture sufficed to assure their acceptance, if not their wholehearted welcome. It was when they began to protest, however politely, their exclusion from the privileges and amenities of those in the inner core that Garfield, at least hesitantly, and Dennett more assertively, came to question their legitimacy as members of the overall student population.

Gaius Charles Bolin got Dennett's message and didn't like what he heard. An attorney in Poughkeepsie, New York, he was the first black graduate of Williams, class of 1889, which lent him great symbolic and moral weight. Bolin was one of numerous black alumni to dispute President Dennett's many and persistent statements that young black men should not be encouraged to seek admission to Williams. John A. Davis '33, then a recent graduate of Williams and later a distinguished psychologist at the City College of New York, carried on a busy correspondence with Dennett in which he argued that Dennett's stand against admitting black students ignored the college's history of educating blacks who had excellent academic records and distinguished careers.

According to Davis, Dennett's stand ignored the role of General Samuel Chapman Armstrong of the class of 1862, the son of missionaries to the Sandwich Islands (later Hawaii) who led black troops in the Civil War and then founded and presided over Hampton Institute following the war. Furthermore, Davis noted, Hampton was only one of numerous colleges designed for the education of freed slaves and their descendants that had been sponsored by the American Missionary Association, whose roots extended to the Haystack Prayer Meeting of 1806.

Bolin himself made clear his disappointment at the college's retreat from equal education. In his letter of October 8, 1936 to O. Dickinson Street, who had been employed to organize a commemoration of the centennial of Mark Hopkins's appointment as president, Bolin sent a check for ten dollars to help pay for the event, but explained that he could not attend in good conscience because of President Dennett's negative attitude regarding the admission of black applicants. Bolin also took Dennett to task for his inconsistent stands on racial and religious discrimination. He noted that Dennett was to be commended as one of forty-one college presidents who had urged the United States to boycott the 1936 Olympics hosted by Nazi Germany because of the German government's discrimination based on race and religion. How, Bolin asked, could Dennett square this action with his views regarding the admission of Negroes to Williams?

The record shows little evidence that Dennett tried, or that he regarded such racial concerns as matters of principle related to the goals of his reforms of the college's fraternity culture. There was an especially revealing exchange of correspondence on the question of admitting black applicants between Dennett and Professor Homer Woodbridge, Williams class of 1902 and a Wesleyan faculty member. Wrote Woodbridge:

> I recognize the force of what you say about the
> handicaps a negro has to face at a college like
> Williams or Wesleyan, and the danger that he
> may get an emotional twist. But he runs that risk
> if he gets educated almost anywhere in America.
> And if you want a college which is representative
> of American life, you can't very well rule out
> negroes any more than you can rule out Jews.
> There will be emotional tensions and complexes,
> no doubt, but they are part of the price that has
> to be paid for the educational values of a student
> body with varied backgrounds.

To Dennett's suggestion that racial fairness would damage Williams' efforts to recruit students from "south of the Mason and Dixon line" who "cannot be brought on to the campus with negroes at this time," Woodbridge replied, "I can't get away from the feeling that for a college to exclude any qualified student on account of his color is un-American. ... I really think a matter of principle is involved."

John Sawyer later observed that a combination of "high principle and low cunning" was essential to presidential success at Williams. His college classmate, James MacGregor Burns, attributed qualities of both lion and fox to Franklin Roosevelt as sources of his transformational leadership. By any measure, Dennett was deficient in the low cunning of the presidential fox.

Pragmatic measures, the willingness to compromise, and the arts of persuasion were unknown to him. He only knew one way to lead, his way. A *Sketch* article vividly described the style and manner that many observers saw in Dennett's presidential role at Williams: "He shouts and thunders and jumps at conclusions; he contradicts himself and seems always sure that Dennett is right. ...He is simple and direct. He is a holy terror. He is human and sincere. He is caustic and inconsiderate."

Add this to the isolation that T. C. Smith observed, and it is no wonder that Dennett failed to achieve many of his goals. Without trusted advisers and unable to build solid coalitions of supporters among the college's constituencies, he did not test his ideas, instincts, and impulses against the judgment and advice of others. Dennett seemed oblivious to the need for reservoirs of good will, understanding, patience, and forgiveness that he could draw upon when wrongheaded instincts and unpopular decisions led to the erosion of popular support.

The nice-boy speech illustrated his vulnerability. The head of admissions, Professor Charles Keller, had been scheduled to visit Exeter Academy two days following Dennett's speech, but Lewis Perry, the head of Exeter and a Williams alumnus and trustee, sent Keller a telegram that read: "I don't know whether you should come up here—we have too many nice boys." Despite his campaign to explain away the offensiveness of the speech, Dennett never regained the support that he needed from students and alumni.

His resignation in 1937, prompted by the board of trustees' purchase of the Greylock Hotel property on North Street, was final proof of the failure of his leadership style. Dennett drew a line in the sand, insisting that in the future all trustee decisions would become effective only with the president's concurrence. When the trustees refused to agree, he had little choice but to resign.

Dennett may have been "the voice of a prophet in the wilderness," as James M. Cole '67 wrote in a paper prepared for an honors course taught by Fred Rudolph, but "the very qualities which fit him to be a prophet prevented him from fulfilling his vision." No one saw more clearly than this president the threat that fraternities posed to the college and its educational mission. He disdained the demands for conformity fraternities imposed on pledges, warning freshmen, "Don't compromise yourself for a mess of pottage." Fraternities, he said, disregarded "the scholastic standing" of pledges, evaluating them only as "social assets." But, he went on, "the college was intended, and is to be, an educational, not a social institution." Fraternities "may cause their own downfall if they do not watch their step." No fraternity could "gain a position of permanent influence on the campus when it is out of line with the fundamental aim of the college."

Such insights would eventually lead to the downfall of fraternities at Williams, but Dennett himself made little progress in reducing their power on campus. Just two years after his resignation, the 1939 yearbook, the *Gul*, introduced the fraternity section with the confident declaration that, "Today, when the fraternity system is firmly entrenched at Williams College and when impressive houses are recognized landmarks of the town, it is difficult to realize that the social system of secret societies has not always been as strong nor as fully accepted as now... ."

Though Dennett should be credited with helping to stimulate a later generation of reformers to free Williams from the shackles of the past, his own brief tenure laid bare and indeed reinforced historical patterns of discrimination that undergirded the fraternity system, while confirming the grip of fraternity culture on undergraduates. Moreover, despite his emphasis on greatly increasing the population of public high school graduates at the college, the proportion of students from boarding schools remained essentially unchanged. Williams was no more like the rest of America than it had been before he arrived.

Dennett understood that his aim of producing "self-made, self reliant, resourceful men" was incompatible with the fraternity culture that prevailed at Williams in the 1930s. Yet his vision seemed incompatible also with modern America. The great theme of Dennett's presidency was the resurrection of the ghost of Mark Hopkins, the centenary of whose presidency was celebrated in 1936. Proclaiming Williams a Christian college, calling for a revival of rugged individualism and the "pioneer spirit," beseeching graduates to shun the temptations of urban life and return to their small towns and villages and provide enlightened leadership there, Dennett seemed to think that Williams, sequestered in a small village in a rural region, could insulate itself from modern complexities.

He ignored historical tides that had reshaped the American cultural landscape considerably during the more than six decades since the end of Hopkins's presidency. Intervening presidents, especially Franklin Carter and Harry Garfield, had been better attuned to those historical tides and attempted to adapt to them in the presidential leadership they provided. Dennett's dual impulses, by contrast, gave impetus to a clash of cultures between the rising forces of modernization and those beholden to the dictates of tradition, between a meritocratic educational culture devoted to rigorous academic standards and the fraternity culture of caste-based privilege and discrimination. The battle would be waged in the decades to come. On its outcome would hang the future of the college, its educational mission, and the character of the graduates Williams sent forth into an ever-changing world.

Chapter 4.
Fraternities Under Siege
1937-1961

James Phinney Baxter '14, a professor of diplomatic history and master of Adams House at Harvard, had declined the offer of the Williams presidency in 1934, when Dennett was appointed. By 1937, Baxter was a member of the Williams board. His fellow trustees approached him again, and this time he accepted the appointment.

Dennett has been justly praised for enlivening the Williams faculty and, like his predecessor, Baxter had a keen eye for faculty talent. Unlike Dennett, the scope of Baxter's vision extended to Jews and others excluded from the faculty rosters of the past. Baxter brought Max Lerner from Harvard, and there followed a steady stream of outstanding Jewish talent that included Emile Despres, Irving Serkin, Kermit Gordon, Irwin Shainman, Fred Greene, and Kurt Tauber.

Phinney Baxter was a significant scholar whose book on the wartime Manhattan Project won the 1947 Pulitzer Prize for history. He stood up courageously for academic freedom when Senator Joe McCarthy and other demagogues were on a crusade to rid colleges of anyone who failed to meet their standards of patriotism. For President Baxter, this meant defending liberal members of the faculty, including Fred Schuman, Robert Brooks, and Max Lerner, against alumni demands that they be fired. Among the faculty, he was admired for his stands on academic freedom and for his humane and generous regard for faculty families suffering from various kinds of hardship and adversity.

In temperament, style, and policy, Baxter offered a sharp contrast with his presidential predecessor. Dennett, for instance, viewed as dangerous the growth of government bureaucracies administering Franklin Roosevelt's New Deal programs designed to revive the economy. He refused federal funds to pay for work

68

scholarships for students from modest circumstances, the very students who were supposed to spearhead his push for diversity at Williams. This led to a highly publicized dispute with Harry Hopkins, the principal architect of Roosevelt's emergency relief programs. When Hopkins addressed a meeting of presidents of land-grant universities in November 1934, he was reported to have remarked that perhaps the attitude of President Dennett reflected that Williams had too much endowment, and maybe an excess of snobbishness as well. Dennett probably did little to counter that perception when he offered this riposte at a campus forum: "As to the assumption that every boy ought to have a college education merely because he wants to go to college, that is pure sentimentalism."

President James Phinney Baxter (1937-1961) saw no reason for change.

"I came with fifteen fraternities and I plan to leave with fifteen."

Though a Republican as Dennett was, Baxter readily accepted financial aid money provided by the New Deal. Following the end of World War II, war veterans who enrolled at Williams brought with them large amounts of federal money for their college expenses under provisions of the G.I. Bill of Rights.

Richard Newhall, along with T. C. Smith, had been pleased in 1934 when Dennett, rather than Baxter, assumed the presidency. But ten years into Baxter's administration, Newhall prepared a memorandum in which he revised his judgments of the two men as presidents. Newhall wrote:

> Becoming increasingly aware of the problems of college administration I have reached the conclusion that Baxter is more successful as a college president.... . He knows better...the nature of the educational problem and the teachers' approach to that problem; at the same time he is more adept, by nature, in being all things to all men, without losing sight of the educational goal. Professors like myself often dislike this, but its practical utility in a world which includes many people who are not professors, is enormous. When in the fall of 1946 Baxter was offered the presidency of Columbia I was appalled at the thought of his leaving Williams.

Newhall's altered perspective on the relative merits of Dennett and Baxter as presidents very likely reflected his own experience in Baxter's role at Williams during World War II. As early as the summer of 1941, Baxter began to divide his time between Williamstown and Washington, a pattern that persisted until 1946. As deputy director of the Office of Strategic Services (OSS), he headed the research and analysis work of that agency. Later, he served as the official historian of the Manhattan Project, which developed the atomic bomb. Newhall, as chairman *pro tempore* of the faculty, served as acting president of the college during Baxter's prolonged absences.

During Baxter's lengthy presidential tenure, fraternities came under great pressure, especially with the enrollment of large numbers of veterans following World War II. He himself was a proud and devoted member of Kappa Alpha and a sentimental man who cherished traditions. When he had been president of the Class of 1914, he spoke out against President Garfield's ban on the caning ceremony, which pitted freshmen and sophomores against one another in a dangerously violent contest. As president, he vowed that he would leave office with the same fifteen fraternities intact that he found upon arrival. He held to his vow, but with great difficulty.

By 1943, when most of the college's facilities had been taken over for training military units, the population of civilian students had declined so sharply that the college closed all fraternities for the duration of the war. Two fraternity kitchens and dining rooms were used to feed regular students, most of them freshmen and sophomores awaiting military orders. As the college returned to its normal order at the end of the war, the influx of veterans that began as a trickle in the autumn of 1945 became a flood by the fall of 1946. Thanks largely to the G.I. Bill, the postwar student body differed greatly from its prewar counterparts. For about five years, the student body was a mix of young civilians just out of high school and military veterans ranging in age from the early to the mid-twenties. Whether or not they had attended Williams before their military service, the war veterans were far more mature, independent, and experienced than the typical pre-war freshman. Many had wives and children. Typically, they had less interest in and knowledge of fraternities. The aims and outcome of World War II fostered an egalitarian and meritocratic spirit that was at odds with the socioeconomic caste system that fraternities symbolized.

Stuart Coan of the class of 1945 typified the changed conditions at the college after the war. "Before I entered military service," Coan wrote "I enjoyed the social aspects of fraternity life without being much involved. After the war when I returned to Williams, I lived in the Phi Gam house and was unhappy with the superficiality and prejudice there, including the exclusion of new members because of their religion." Coan added that he "joined Phi Gamma Delta as a 'legacy' because my father [Frank Coan, class of 1911] had been a member of Alpha Zeta Alpha, a local fraternity which later became Phi Gam."

Frank Coan's Williams experience had been very different from his son's. "My father was devoted to Williams largely because it was his home while his parents were missionaries in Persia during his four years. The AZA house was central to his college life at a time when fraternities strongly encouraged self-improvement and social service. He was very proud that AZA had a number of outstanding members." These included Herbert Lehman, Morris Ernst, and Francis Sayre, later High Commissioner in the Philippines, as well as two classmates who became Williams trustees, Abbott Mills and Jay Angevine. Coan's description of his father's experience helps explain why many alumni of earlier generations were so profoundly attached to the college's fraternity culture.

The changed student demography led President Baxter and the trustees in 1946 to establish the Committee on Post-War Extra-Curricular Activities, which came to be known as the Shriver Committee. The Shriver Committee membership included President Baxter, three additional administrative officers, one faculty member, two trustees, and twenty-two alumni. Among the college's major constituencies, students were conspicuously absent from the committee. Fraternities had been closed since 1943 because of the war, and the central purpose of the committee was to determine under what conditions fraternity operations would be resumed when they re-opened in 1947. The changed campus ethos that led to the creation of the committee is suggested by a *Williams Record* editorial from September 27, 1946. "We do not want to return to 'normalcy,' if by normalcy is meant the days of carefree irresponsibility and lack of concern for anything beyond the next houseparty, the next drink, or the next trip to Smith. We want the post-war Williams to have its fun, but we want that fun to be a secondary feature in college life."

The Shriver Committee recommended, though with a large dissenting minority, that fraternity rushing be deferred until sophomore year, which would require a new dining space for freshmen, and that a new space be provided to strengthen the Garfield Club.

These recommendations were designed to weaken the hold of fraternities on the college's culture, but the committee fell far short of suggesting the end of fraternities or other radical changes. Even so, President Baxter and the trustees were not ready for the reforms the committee called for. They simply let the recommendations die, thus tacitly siding with the committee minority. Their inaction also reflected worry about costs associated with the proposed changes. Those financial concerns were realistic, as Williams still trailed Amherst in its endowment.

Yet, the agitation for change continued, and, in 1951, the Committee on Campus Problems was appointed. Dykeman Sterling '29 chaired the committee of about forty members, including trustees and alumni, faculty, and students, which came to be known by the name of its chairman. With more conviction and little dissent within its ranks, the Sterling Committee recommended many of the changes advocated by the Shriver Committee, among them deferring rushing until the sophomore year and new facilities for freshmen dining and the Garfield Club, needs that would be met by the building of Baxter Hall in 1953-1954.

The committee, however, voted down a proposal to break the fraternity grip on feeding students by providing central dining for all students, as Amherst had done with the construction of Valentine Hall in 1941. It also refused to endorse a proposal that would have ensured fraternity membership for any student wishing to join, a policy that would come to be known as "total opportunity."

The president and trustees approved the Sterling Committee's proposals for deferred rushing, the construction of a student union, and new quarters for the Garfield Club, and it appeared these changes were about to be made. However, members of the Garfield Club had other thoughts. The combination of approval of new quarters for their club and the rejection of an open membership policy for fraternities prompted the Garfield Club's members, some 190 strong, to vote, on December 5, 1951, to disband their organization unless by the spring semester—less than two months away—all students were free to join a fraternity. Members of the Garfield Club refused to be implicit accomplices in what they perceived to be a ruse that would perpetuate indefinitely an essentially unchanged fraternity system.

73

The Garfield Club's threat presented a difficult dilemma for President Baxter. A regular meeting of the faculty on December 17, 1951, devoted two hours to those matters. Professor James MacGregor Burns '39, who as an undergraduate had been president of the Garfield Club and now served as faculty adviser to the organization, began the discussion by reading the following statement, which he offered as a motion for faculty approval:

> The decision of the Garfield Club no longer to support present social arrangements has produced a critical situation at Williams College. The Faculty has recognized the increasing seriousness of the cleavage between fraternity and non-fraternity groups and we consider the action of the Club a natural result of the evils of the present social system. We commend the Club for taking decisive steps to emphasize the existence of these evils and to press for reform. We are convinced that the dissolution of the Club without forthright action to correct the social system will produce an intolerable situation at Williams, one that will be as destructive to life inside the community as it will be damaging to the College's reputation outside.

Burns then noted that the Garfield Club's principal demand was that "all students be guaranteed an invitation to fraternity membership" and he urged adoption of that proposal. He also advocated serious consideration of "a College House Plan" of residential organization, which, if adopted, would, presumably, supersede fraternities and thus mean their abolition.

President Baxter pushed back against the Burns proposals, arguing that forcing an open membership policy against strong opposition of the fraternities would jeopardize student, alumni, and trustee support for deferred rushing and the building of a student union. After amendments stripped away the references to open membership and the commendation of a house plan of residential organization, Burns's original motion

74

passed overwhelmingly. Burns at that point moved that the faculty's action be widely publicized. Baxter, in response, noted that he was unaware of instances in which a faculty resolution was published before submission to the trustees, and Burns's motion was defeated.

"The Faculty has recognized the increasing seriousness of the cleavage between fraternity and non-fraternity groups," Professor James Macgregor Burns '39 commented, "and we consider the action of the [Garfield] Club a natural result of the evils of the present social system."

Following the Christmas recess that began shortly after the faculty meeting, faculty and students brought strong pressure upon the administration to put the open membership question to the student body. A hastily arranged referendum in January 1952, with 90 percent of students participating, resulted in 509 opposed to open membership and 390 in favor. About half of the favorable votes came from Garfield Club members. Afterwards, President Baxter reiterated that, if fraternity undergraduates and alumni chose to adopt open membership for their chapters, they were free to do so, but the trustees would not impose such a system on them. For its part, the Garfield Club fulfilled its vow when president Harold Kahn '52 announced on January 31, 1952, the immediate dissolution of the club.

The end of freshman rushing in 1954 substantially changed the dynamics of student life. It strengthened class cohesion, as did having all freshmen dine together. On the other hand, the walling off of freshmen from upper class students so as to prevent "dirty rushing" (violations of college rules that forbade fraternity members from contacting new students before the stipulated rush period) had the undesirable effect of making even more pronounced the division of the campus into a multiplicity of residential enclaves, each with its own culture.

Deferred rushing also intensified the status stratification of fraternities because fraternities and freshmen students alike had much more time and opportunity to size up one another before making decisions. And because the ban on pledging freshmen meant that all fraternities were forced to pledge more upper classmen to meet their expenses, the less popular fraternities faced mounting financial woes. Indeed, the college administration offered struggling fraternities assistance in managing their finances by such measures as joint purchase plans for food and other essential commodities.

A number of fraternities were limited in their recruiting in this period of intensified rushing by secret covenants imposed by their nationals that forbade the pledging of students from particular racial or religious groups, mainly Jews and blacks. In addition, blackballs and other forms of veto that allowed individuals and small groups to block nominations for any (or no) reason continued as part of the culture of most fraternities. All of these circumstances deepened the financial problems of some fraternities, leading to fears of bankruptcy. That failed to materialize because vulnerable fraternities opened their doors even wider and increasingly defied the demands of their national bodies regarding groups that were judged inadmissible. As the fraternities inched their way ever closer to open membership in fact as well as theory, they approached the goal that the Garfield Club had vainly sought.

When, in 1957, the fraternities themselves proposed total opportunity, the administration accepted the plan and announced that it would take effect with the fall 1960 rushing season. In fact, however, fraternities went ahead immediately with efforts to achieve total opportunity. Financial pressures meant that they could not afford to wait.

By moving ahead of the administration, fraternities could better control the ground rules for total opportunity. Even before deferred rushing and total opportunity, there was wide variation in the policies by which fraternities judged who was admissible and who was not. It is important to understand that the voluntary acceptance of total opportunity was a collective commitment that allowed individual fraternities to continue discriminatory practices, and some did. Thus, the membership opportunity was less than total, and not surprisingly, the system did not always function as anticipated.

Fraternity officers thought initially that they could work their way through this thicket by requiring every fraternity to list in order of preference all members of the sophomore class. Correspondingly, all members of the class who wished to rush were supposed to list all fifteen fraternities in order of preference. These data were then fed into a computer, which would spit out answers concerning who would go to which fraternity. Or so it was assumed. Sometimes it worked and sometimes it did not. When it didn't work—most often when students listed fewer than fifteen fraternities—a residual group of students was left out in the cold. The house officers then had the unenviable task of working their way through the list of rejects and dividing them up. This process was sometimes referred to as the "turkey shoot." Despite these drawbacks, total opportunity was working well enough within a few years that discrimination against Jewish students diminished markedly, and black students, the last group to suffer seriously from discrimination, were able to become fraternity members of some houses even while other fraternities continued the practice of not offering bids to blacks.

Some alumni were infuriated by this method of choosing members of fraternities. Eugene Hoyne '07 threatened to stop total opportunity with a lawsuit. He argued assigning membership to persons who were not elected by those already in the brotherhood effectively nullified the very meaning of fraternity and violated the constitutional right of freedom of association. He was essentially correct in perceiving that total opportunity was a significant step toward the abolition of fraternities. He dropped the effort to block it when he learned that it had been an initiative of the fraternities themselves, not the administration or trustees.

In retrospect, it can be seen that the pre-war fraternity system with its pecking order and intense student engagement resembled Humpty Dumpty in that it could never be put back together again. The mystique and authority by which fraternities had disciplined and influenced the behavior of their members were greatly diminished. The notion of upholding the honor of one's fraternity came to mean far less, and some houses seemed to take a perverse pride in "animal house" reputations. Many fraternities abandoned at least some of their rituals or reduced them to mocking parodies. Faculty members and students who served on the Discipline Committee were aware of the frequency and seriousness of cases involving fraternities. Though the *Williams Record* sometimes carried stories about such incidents, alumni, by and large, had an outdated perception of fraternities.

It did not help the case for fraternities that in May 1957 the Williams College Council Committee on Discrimination issued a report, unofficially known as the Phillips Report after the committee's student chairman, David Phillips '58, which revealed that three houses had unwritten agreements with their national bodies that forbade the pledging of African Americans, and two had similar agreements regarding Jewish students. The Phillips Report, which the *Alumni Review* published in its July 1957 issue, offered a comprehensive analysis of the patterns of discrimination in the processes by which Williams fraternities chose their members. The statistics in the report covered the years 1950-1956, shortly before the beginning of total opportunity. These data were supplemented by information gathered through interviews of fraternity members. The Phillips Report, in short, sought to measure the realities of the fraternity selection processes against the trustee position that fraternities should choose members strictly on the basis of individual ability, achievement, character, and personality.

The college possessed information on the religious affiliations of students, information that was gathered after they had matriculated. A reassuring conclusion of the Phillips Report was that for the period in question (1950-1956), there was no evidence of fraternity discrimination against Roman Catholic students. In view of earlier evidence of widespread discrimination against Catholics, particularly those with Italian and Irish origins, this was encouraging news.

With regard to Jewish students, the findings were mixed, with signs of progress but also problems to be addressed. The report summarized the overall picture as follows:

> Two unwritten agreements with national fraternity organizations clearly exist to the exclusion of Jewish students. Only one of these is carried out in practice at the present time. Of the other thirteen houses at the present time, the committee has found four which can be described as having segments in their membership which act to prevent the pledging of Jewish students as a group. Of these four houses two have had no Jewish students over this six-year period and two have [pledged Jews during that period.]. Of the four only one has a Jewish student at the present time.

The committee forcefully noted that the central problem of fraternity discrimination against Jewish students was not total exclusion from membership but rather denial of equal opportunity for membership. A pervasive theme in the interviews of fraternity members was a concern about limiting the number of final bids offered to Jews. Interestingly, alumni members, who generally did not become involved with the selection of new pledges, often did urge limits on Jewish members. This preoccupation seems to have been rooted in concern over the general perception of the fraternity. In any event, the result was that Jewish students, on average, received significantly fewer bids than non-Jews. It was also true, however, that, following the adoption of deferred rushing in 1952, fraternities began to offer many more bids to Jews as a part of the general movement to pledge more members for budget reasons. The fact that Jewish members were becoming house presidents and holding other offices indicated a hopeful trend that was gaining momentum.

79

In assessing the question of fraternity discrimination against blacks, it is important to understand that Williams continued to enroll very few Negroes (the term used in the report). Generally, the number of African Americans enrolled at the college at any given time was well under ten. Still, as indicated by the experience of Clinton Knox '30 and his friends referred to earlier, as well as Tyler Dennett's well-publicized attitude toward the admission of blacks, there was an institutional history, consistent with a long national history, that had a bearing on attitudes at Williams in the 1950s.

While the overall tone of the Phillips Report indicated growing acceptance of Jewish pledges, the notion of accepting black members clearly stirred apprehension and resistance. Consider the following statement from the report: "Six houses have contacted their local alumni group within recent years in reference to the possibility of pledging a Negro. Of these six, four Alumni groups expressed their disapproval of such a move. ... All of these four houses had southern chapters and this fact was a definite consideration when disapproval was voiced." According to the report, two fraternities that chose to pledge black students had been expelled by their nationals. Still, despite the outside influences that induced caution and apprehension regarding the possibility of pledging African Americans, the most important barriers remained the attitudes of current undergraduate members. It is perhaps surprising to read that: "The committee feels justified in concluding from the information gathered in its interviews that even in those few houses where outside influences are especially negligible the undergraduate membership at this time would not pledge a Negro."

One exception was Sigma Phi, which in 1956 pledged two black students, Ted Wynne and Bill George, thus becoming the first Williams fraternity to break through that barrier. When the Sigma Phi pledge class for the following year declined by almost half, that development was widely viewed as the price paid by Sigma Phi for its courageous action. Two years following Sigma Phi's election of black members, however, total opportunity was in effect, and fraternities were feeling the financial pinch resulting from deferred rushing. With a rushing program led by vice president Wynne, the Sigma Phi pledge class was back to its former level.

The constitution of the Phi Gamma Delta national fraternity had a provision that forbade local chapters to pledge anyone who "was not acceptable to the fraternity as a whole." That language was understood to refer to Jews and blacks. As noted earlier, Phi Gamma Delta had an unusual history at Williams. It received a charter from the national organization in 1880, but suspended operations almost at once. It was revived in 1913 when a local fraternity, Alpha Zeta Alpha, was awarded Phi Gamma Delta's charter and name. Alpha Zeta Alpha had pledged Jews from its beginning in 1903, and that practice continued under its new identity. Apparently the Phi Gamma Delta national officers chose to ignore this conflict with its constitution, but, in 1958, the president of the college's chapter, Carl Vogt '58, a future president of Williams, received a seemingly ominous invitation, accompanied by an air travel ticket, to journey to Washington and meet with the trustees of the national organization to discuss the constitutional requirement regarding selection of members.

Vividly recalling these events almost fifty-five years later, Vogt reported that the chair of the trustees "put the question directly to me about my chapter's position on pledging a Negro. I told him that if a Negro whom we liked came through rush that we would pledge him." The follow-up question to Vogt was what he would do if pledging a Negro were unacceptable to the national organization. "I told them that if I was president (and I assumed that it would also be true for my successors), I would lead the chapter out of the national fraternity. In my case, I already had the support of the members."

To Vogt's surprise, the trustees smiled with seeming relief at his response. It became clear that the national trustees were primarily worried about the Amherst chapter, which had given notice that it was prepared to mount a public campaign to pledge a black member. The national trustees were apparently concerned that the Amherst chapter might carry its fight to the floor of the annual meeting of the national organization and that Williams might be allied with that effort. Vogt indicated that the Williams chapter felt little attachment to the national and paid scant attention to its requirements. For his part, Vogt was left with the impression that the Williams chapter could chart its own course without interference as long as it did not openly challenge the national.

The findings of the Phillips Report that Williams fraternities practiced active and deeply-rooted discrimination were sobering and embarrassing, though they confirmed assumptions already widely accepted. The report received considerable national attention, including a prominent article in the July 7, 1957, issue of the *New York Times*. This publicity led to many requests from other campuses and various organizations for copies of the report. Soon after its release, Williams trustees set a September 15, 1960, deadline for house presidents to declare in writing that their houses were free of any discriminatory agreements.

The officers of the Gargoyle Alumni Association perceived that Williams was in a very vulnerable position at that time. Election to the Gargoyle Society during that era was a greatly prized honor. Membership was based upon campus leadership and implied a lifetime obligation to provide leadership whenever Williams faced unusual opportunities or threats. By 1960, three developments had come together to create a potential crisis for the college: the revelations in the Phillips Report; the challenge of meeting the commitment to total opportunity; and the looming September 15, 1960, deadline for fraternity officers to submit letters to President Baxter assuring him that "the chapter is free to elect to membership any individual on the basis of his merit as a person."

Gargoyle Alumni President Donald Fuchs '44 appointed a committee consisting of Dickinson R. Debevoise '46, Robert J. Geniesse '51, and David S. Maclay '42. Their task was to prepare a report that, informed by meetings with undergraduate leaders of fraternities, would instruct and guide the students responsible for fraternity rushing. Fuchs's successor as president of the Gargoyle Alumni Association, Rhett Austell '48, presented the report on

July 15, 1960, just two months before Baxter's deadline for non-discrimination pledges.

Coming to the heart of the issue, the Gargoyle report stated:

> If the system of total opportunity which has been agreed to is to become a reality next Fall, it will require the acceptance for membership in fraternities of three Negro students who will be participating in rushing with the rest of the sophomore class. Thus, the test of the fraternities' determination to make total opportunity work, will at the same time be construed as a test of their willingness to admit Negro students to membership and of the success of the policy of the Board of Trustees that there shall be no restrictions that compel fraternities to exclude men because of their race, creed, or color.... [S]ince all of the fraternities operate under a system by which one or a few members can block the admission of any student, the solution of the problem rests primarily with the undergraduate members of the fraternities.

The report sternly warned that if the fraternities failed to carry out their agreement to accept all students who wished to join, including black students, the reputation of Williams stood to suffer serious damage from the news coverage that would attend rushing in the coming autumn. The report took hopeful note that undergraduate fraternity officers were in the process of negotiating agreements intended to achieve the rushing outcomes to which they were committed, but with no assurances that those negotiations would be successful. It concluded with an appeal to alumni to avoid any intervention that would interfere with the success of total opportunity.

It is not possible to overemphasize the threat identified by the report of the Gargoyle Alumni Association. Its authors perceived that, amidst the seemingly carefully contrived guarantees that all students would be able to join a fraternity,

83

there were ticking time bombs in the form of fraternity bylaws that permitted individual undergraduate members or small groups of members to veto nominations for membership. Rhett Austell '48 and other alumni of that general era had the impression, decades after fraternities were gone, that there were varying degrees of awareness in the houses that such bylaws existed, and diverse histories regarding the actual use of such vetoes. But the possibility that the threat would materialize hung ominously over the college.

Dickinson Debevoise '46:
"We can't stay where we are, and we can't go backwards."

   The spring of 1957 saw not only the Phillips Report on discrimination but also a radical proposal issued by a group of students who called themselves the Committee of 22 but were quickly dubbed the "Terrible 22." They offered a searing critique of fraternities and advocated their total elimination, to be replaced by a social system based upon the random assignment of students to residential units by the college administration. This group's proposals foreshadowed the recommendations of the Angevine Committee in 1962 that would effectively end fraternities.

In 1957, however, President Baxter promptly rejected the recommendations of the Terrible 22 as unrealistic. The majority of students, perhaps influenced by hostile articles in the *Williams Record*, were no less dismissive. Strong support came only from the faculty, but the report stirred much discussion and set the stage for the actions that ensued almost immediately when President John Sawyer took office.

Chapter 5.
The Sawyer Revolution
1961-1973

As a senior in 1939, John E. Sawyer wrote an honors thesis under the supervision of President Baxter. So impressed was Baxter by Sawyer and his work that thereafter he frequently spoke of his student as a probable future Williams president. When Sawyer was appointed to the board of trustees at the unusually young age of thirty-four, the rumor that he was being groomed to succeed Baxter became widespread. Jack Sawyer's widow, Anne Sawyer, remembered years later that, when her husband attended his first Williams board meeting in 1952, he was embarrassed at President Baxter's introduction of him as the likely next president of Williams.

When the time came for choosing Baxter's successor, however, it was apparent that relations between the two men had cooled. As a trustee, Sawyer was outspoken about the college's languid fundraising efforts and the lack of attention to the curriculum, the basic structure of which had remained unchanged since 1911 and was out of step with developments at many other colleges. Just as important, Sawyer had openly disagreed with Baxter's cautious response to fraternity issues.

Meanwhile, Baxter signaled that his preferred candidate as successor was Vincent M. Barnett, a highly respected Williams political science professor who oversaw the Marshall Plan in Italy following World War II. A decision to name him would have pleased many of his faculty colleagues, but he was not a Williams alumnus, and the trustees had not gone outside alumni ranks for a president since the appointment of Edward Dorr Griffin in 1821.

Far fewer faculty members knew Sawyer, an associate professor of economics at Yale. His graduate study at Harvard had been interrupted by service in World War II. Upon returning to

86

Harvard, he was elected a junior member of the Society of Fellows, an elite subset of the Harvard faculty; election to membership required exceptional scholarly distinction. The junior fellowship program was designed to develop scholars whose work would transcend narrow disciplinary boundaries and, in Sawyer's case, the appointment opened up extraordinary opportunities for study with preeminent Harvard scholars in a variety of fields. His intellectual interests were wide-ranging, and his junior fellow status enabled him to broaden and deepen his knowledge. That he never completed his Ph.D. was not unusual. At least in Harvard circles, election to the Society of Fellows was regarded as perhaps even more prestigious than earning a Ph.D.

Still, his thin record of published scholarship undoubtedly contributed to Sawyer's failure to achieve tenure at Harvard after he was appointed to the economics department, and perhaps explained why he was not a full professor at Yale when the Williams search committee turned to him. He lacked another usual credential, in that he had never held an academic administrative position. He appeared to be a cautious, conservative man whose election as president would portend little in the way of change. What, then, commended him to the Williams board?

The trustees were, of course, well acquainted with fraternity issues, but there is no evidence that they wanted a president who would chart a radically new direction for Williams. After all, a solid majority of them had followed Baxter's lead in resisting the more far-reaching proposals regarding reform of fraternity practices. A more likely factor in Sawyer's favor was that he and his wife had numerous family connections with the college; he was deeply steeped in Williams history and traditions.

Another qualification would appear to have been his reputation as an exceptionally able administrator outside of academia, as evidenced by his wartime work in the Office of Strategic Services, the precursor of the CIA. It was not by chance that Sawyer, who was commissioned a Navy lieutenant in 1942, was assigned to the OSS, where he worked in Washington under Baxter in the research and analysis division of the OSS. Following his Washington assignment, Sawyer was posted to Algeria during the struggle between the Allied and Axis powers for control of North Africa. After the Allied invasion of Europe, he was sent to Paris to head the research and analysis work of the OSS for all of Western Europe. He oversaw the work of approximately ninety subordinates, many of them considerably older than he. As Baxter had sensed early on and as his OSS experience demonstrated, Sawyer's temperament was that of the activist intellectual who would find fulfillment and eventually leave an impact on history by putting ideas to work in the world of practical affairs. In retrospect, it was fortunate that the Williams trustees recognized his leadership potential.

When John Sawyer first arrived at his desk in Hopkins Hall in 1961, a message awaited him from a group of forty-five students that would define his presidency. The so-called Grinnell petition had originally gone to President Baxter less than a month before his retirement. It came at a time that, as Fred Rudolph wrote, "the College's reputation had been sliding and that a widespread impression was abroad that Williams had been stalled."

The petition grew out of discussions within a student group organized by Bruce Grinnell '62. It asked the president and the trustees to form a committee to seek alternatives to the fraternity membership selection process. The statement warned that failure to act on the petition would lead the fraternity members among the signers to resign from their fraternities and demand that the college provide them living and dining accommodations. Because the petition signers were virtually all campus leaders who could command a following, and because the college was heavily dependent upon fraternities to feed and house upper class students, that threat was serious. Grinnell, co-captain and quarterback of the football team, a Junior Adviser, and a member of Gargoyle, was also president of Alpha Delta Phi, arguably the most prestigious fraternity on campus.

Against the background of numerous and far-reaching reform efforts, beginning just after World War II and including the changes in the fraternity membership selection process that had come about since 1957, the Grinnell petition may appear to have been an odd demand, a demand that begged the question of what further reform measures were possible or needed. After all, the fraternities themselves had proposed universal access in 1957 and, by 1961, it was generally accepted that any student who wanted to be in a fraternity would receive at least one bid. It was also in 1957 that the Phillips Report, after a thorough investigation, identified those Williams fraternities whose national bodies secretly imposed unwritten membership prohibitions based upon religious or racial criteria. By the time the Grinnell petition arrived in Hopkins Hall, President Baxter and the trustees had already demanded and received assurance from all fraternities that such exclusionary agreements would not be permitted at Williams.

The students who drew up the petition had at least a vague sense of this history and, in a general way, they also knew the dirty secret—hidden in plain view—that had deeply concerned the officers of the Gargoyle Alumni Association. The Gargoyle report of July 15, 1960, pointedly underscored the vulnerability of the college because "all of the fraternities operate under a system by which one or a few members can block the admission of any student... ." The juxtaposition of those bylaws with commitments to open membership made by the president, trustees, and the fraternities themselves meant the fraternity membership selection process amounted to little more than an uneasy truce.

For about four years following the adoption of total opportunity, Williams lucked out, in the sense that by one means or another all students who wanted to be in a fraternity had that opportunity. The elaborate membership selection mechanism that had brought about that result was a contraption worthy of the imagination of Rube Goldberg, since the annual effort to achieve total opportunity involved various inducements to win the cooperation of fraternities. Increased house membership quotas were sometimes used as a reward for fraternities that were willing to extend bids to students who appeared to be in danger of receiving no bids.

The string of luck ran out in the spring of 1961 when three of Bruce Grinnell's Alpha Delta Phi brothers used a chapter bylaw to block the election of a Korean student, Myong-Ku (Charlie) Ahn '63. Grinnell, the president of Alpha Delta Phi, had proposed the election of Ahn at the urging of another member of the fraternity, Robert Seidman '63. Ahn's election appeared certain because he was already well known as a social member of the house. Social membership, a category used by some but not all fraternities, allowed a few students to attend parties and dine at the house but did not permit them to room there or attend chapter meetings. Ahn was also an excellent student who later received a Ph.D. in chemistry from Yale. Grinnell was stunned when Ahn's nomination was defeated by what was generally known as "buttering," which permitted as few as three members to block a nomination under the provisions of an Alpha Delta bylaw. They needed only to state, in effect, "I like him well enough, but... ." A buttering verdict was generally understood to mean that the opponents of a nomination did not feel comfortable with the proposed member as an addition to the brotherhood, in a setting that was similar to that of a family. Such a candidate failed the oft-quoted test, "Would I like for him to date or marry my sister?"

Grinnell acknowledged, many years later, that he had little awareness of the reform efforts that had preceded his initiative. And he did not view his action as another step in that long history. However, after encountering the realities of the fraternity selection process when the victim was Charlie Ahn, he instinctively recognized its inherent evil and the great injury it inflicted. Having checked with officers of other fraternities and confirmed that such bylaws were commonplace, Grinnell had acted, and he quickly learned that others were prepared to join in demanding an end to such practices.

Grinnell and his colleagues did not call for the abolition of fraternities. Indeed, they clearly assumed their continuation. They were, however, urging that the determination of fraternity membership be through administrative decisions, not student elections. With respect to fraternity issues, the history of Williams illustrated an incremental, gradualist approach. The reports and studies of the previous fifteen years had been critical of fraternities and advocated changes, many of them adopted, but all had assumed that fraternities would remain a powerful presence on campus. Both the student petitioners and the new president appear to have implicitly assumed a continuation of that history.

Yet the outcome of the Grinnell Petition would be different. The result was not reform but a revolution, not an increment but a great leap. The unwitting launch of a radical change started with the actions of petitioners with impeccable fraternity credentials, men who, like Grinnell, were leaders in their houses.

The fraternity credentials of the petition's recipient were also ideal. John Sawyer had been president of Zeta Psi, as had his brother William H. (Bill) Sawyer '37, and his father William H. Sawyer '08. While that history gave him room to maneuver, his OSS background encouraged him to think strategically. In plotting a course of action, he was very careful about process; typically, he was several moves ahead of everyone else. He viewed the Grinnell petition as a strategic opportunity. He decided to seize the moment to address a problem that he saw as a serious liability for Williams, even if, at the outset, he was uncertain about where he wanted this particular initiative to emerge.

Consistent with the approach that President Baxter had taken in appointing the Shriver Committee and then the Sterling Committee, Sawyer's first step was to create the Committee of Review on Fraternity Questions. That he followed Baxter's example signaled to many that the history of incremental reform would continue under the new president. He dictated no mandate, defined no outcome, and specified no remedy for the issues that concerned the student petitioners. Instead, he took enough care in appointing committee members that he could be assured that they would act in the best interests of Williams and not propose measures that would be irresponsible or unwise.

As chairman of the committee, Sawyer appointed Jay Angevine '11, a prominent Boston attorney who had recently stepped down as a trustee. Joining Angevine were eleven others.

They included another recently retired trustee, Michael Griggs '44, a New York advertising executive; two current trustees, John Osborne '25, a Chicago businessman, and Ferdinand Thun '30, a textiles manufacturer; two faculty members, William Gates '39, an economist, and chemistry professor J. Hodge Markgraf '52, the non-voting secretary of the committee; two students, Bruce Grinnell '62 and Robert Durham '62; and four additional alumni, Edward Stanley '37, an insurance executive, and three attorneys, Frederic Nathan '43, Dickinson Debevoise '46, and Robert Geniesse '51. Nathan was the only non-fraternity member on the committee, and he, along with Debevoise, and Geniesse, had served on the Sterling Committee. Attentive as he was to process, Sawyer looked especially to the lawyers to ensure that decision-making would be subject to orderly procedures. Taken together, the four attorneys on the committee represented an impressive array of legal talent.

Jay Angevine '11 observed, "If fraternities can reclaim their former virtue, more power to them.... . There are many fraternal organizations that achieve distinction without any dependence on bed and board."

With these committee members, Sawyer could be confident that decisions about the future would be informed by first-hand knowledge of both the sobering realities of Greek life and the positive features reflected in its long history at Williams. Angevine, for instance, was a member of Phi Gamma Delta, the fraternity of Herbert Lehman and Morris Ernst. He was well aware that, despite its storied past, his fraternity had had a more recent history of serious disciplinary problems.

One episode, in 1958, received considerable attention both on and off the campus. A few days before commencement when there were few students besides seniors on campus, a party at Phi Gamma Delta drew many members of other houses. After an evening of pornographic movies and heavy drinking, a large crowd went across the street and badly damaged a wood-frame dormitory that had been part of the old Greylock Hotel. With his trustees in town for commencement weekend, an angry President Baxter informed the Phi Gamma Delta seniors that they would not graduate unless they paid immediately for the vandalism.

Trustee Ferdinand Thun '30 was the father of Peter Thun '59 and thus could draw upon his son's knowledge of the current conditions in fraternities. John Osborne '25, had two sons at Williams (both were Chi Psis) while the committee was doing its work. Another committee member who was widely known and respected among alumni had a Williams son who was in deep academic trouble, largely because of over-investment in fraternity activities, and subsequently flunked out. Sterling Committee veterans Nathan, Debevoise, and Geniesse were thoroughly acquainted with issues relating to fraternities during the post-World War II period.

The committee convened it first meeting in October 1961 and delivered its report on May 5, 1962, following a total of eight meetings of the full committee, five on the Williams campus and three at the Williams Club in New York. In a speech Angevine would give to Alumni Fund class agents on October 6, 1962, he described the phasing of the committee's work during its seven-month lifespan. According to Angevine's account, the committee was occupied through the fall and winter and into the early spring with appeals to groups and individuals to provide testimony, meetings to hear that testimony, and inquiries into practices on other campuses. Then, as he put it, the shades came down. The committee privately discussed what it had learned, and individual members submitted statements of their own position on the issues at hand. Then came the arduous task, led by Angevine himself, of drafting a report for the trustees.

Bruce Grinnell '62, President of Alpha Delta Phi and an Eph football captain, led a student group to petition the president and trustees when his own fraternity refused to admit a Korean student, Myong-Ku Ahn '63. The result was a chain of events that led to the abolition of fraternities.

When the committee began its proceedings in the fall of 1961, it was by no means a certainty that it would recommend an end to the role that fraternities had played at Williams for almost a century and a third. As Fred Nathan '43, the only non-affiliate member of the committee, would write, "I recall vividly the first meeting of the Angevine Committee, which was held at the Williams Club in New York City. Jay asked each of the members to state his position. There was a total range of answers, from extremely pro to extremely con, and I feared that we were in for a long slog with an uncertain outcome."

Given the history of other reform efforts, many on campus were skeptical that large initiatives would emerge from the committee's work. The surprising fact that only about thirty persons spoke before the committee, despite multiple appeals for testimony, attested to a perceived indifference and a general expectation that fraternities would go on as before. Indeed, time would tell that a large majority of students were not ready for dramatic changes. Grinnell and his classmate Robert Durham, the two student representatives, recalled that after their initial exposure to the other committee members, they themselves were

94

doubtful that anything significant would result from the deliberations.

When asked almost fifty years later about the internal dynamics of the committee and how it arrived at a consensus, Durham confirmed Nathan's memory that, at the outset, committee members appeared to be sharply divided about fraternities. Some of the older members, including John Osborne '25 and Edward Stanley '37, seemed troubled and perplexed that there were questions about whether fraternities were good for Williams and worried that Grinnell and Durham were unrealistically idealistic. The civil rights movement was stirring the nation, and students at Williams, as elsewhere, were acutely aware of those events. Thompson Chapel had been filled to overflowing with students when Martin Luther King Jr. preached there in April 1961, just as Grinnell and his group were discussing and drafting their petition. The petitioners knew about former chaplain William Sloane Coffin's sermons and discussions that addressed fraternity discrimination. Within a couple of years, almost forty Williams students would be with King in Birmingham in the ranks of the Freedom Marchers.

Durham recalled two moments in particular that nudged committee members toward a consensus on the need to act. One was the occasion when only two students appeared before the committee to make the case for fraternities, despite strong appeals for such testimony, and neither offered persuasive arguments.

The second event, Durham reported, occurred after the committee began its private deliberations following the gathering of testimony. Dickinson Debevoise presented a position paper that had a galvanizing effect on his committee colleagues. Debevoise at that time was a young lawyer. Later he would volunteer his legal services to Martin Luther King Jr. and become an important figure in efforts to resolve the issues that had produced racial turmoil and widespread arson in Newark, New Jersey, in 1967. When asked in 2011 about Durham's recollection of his role in the committee's deliberations, Debevoise, by then a highly regarded federal judge, appointed decades earlier by President Carter, shared with the author the position paper to which Durham had referred. That document had provided the committee his view of where it stood and how it might move to a conclusion.

Fred Nathan '43: "I feared that we were in for a long slog with an uncertain outcome."

Summarizing information collected by the committee, Debevoise incisively described the inherent differences and incompatibilities between the character and purposes of a fraternity and those of a liberal arts college. He noted that for over a century Williams had acquiesced as fraternities assumed a large role in the school's residential, social, and dining life. Yet, he argued, the college must be held accountable for the results. The final responsibility for determining the residential and social arrangements that would be most supportive of the college's educational aims, Debevoise concluded, must lie with the trustees and administration, rather than with alumni fraternity corporations, house officers, and the national fraternity organizations. Otherwise, as committee chair Angevine would later put it, fifteen fraternities and Williams College—in effect sixteen separate colleges—shared the management of life at the 450-acre campus in Williamstown. The measures that resulted from the recommendations of the Sterling Committee, Debevoise went on, had recognized the priority of the college's educational mission. Deferred rushing, a product of that committee's work, had created great problems for fraternities. Total opportunity exacerbated those problems to such a degree that, in order to guarantee the viability of fraternities, those two fundamental changes in fraternity life would have to be reversed. That was plainly unacceptable. An attempt to maintain the fraternity status quo of 1961-1962 would result in recurring crises of the sort that had become commonplace in recent years. Debevoise concluded, "We can't stay where we are, and we can't go backwards."

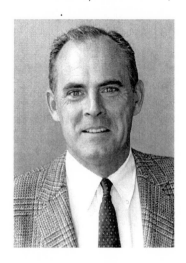

In response to President Sawyer's suggestion that the Angevine Committee had gone too far, William Gates '39 offered, "Maybe so, but now it's too late; we have reached our conclusions."

According to Durham, Debevoise's statement produced a palpable sense of relief around the table. Gone was the temptation to wriggle away from the conclusion that the committee must deal forthrightly with a problem that was no longer amenable to temporizing fixes. Still, an apparent consensus for action did not yet lead to a similar agreement on how to act.

Jack Sawyer never met with the committee as a whole, and both he and Jay Angevine said later that they discussed the committee's work only once. But the body of testimony that Sawyer himself provided over the years, combined with various Angevine Committee documents, demonstrated that Sawyer had significant exchanges with committee members Jay Angevine and William Gates '39 during the crucial period from February to the submission of the report to the trustees on May 5, 1962. These

97

exchanges and other documents in the Williams College archives show the committee's thinking as it evolved toward unanimous agreement on actions to take.

In a letter to President Sawyer dated February 16, 1962, Jay Angevine enclosed a preliminary draft of a committee report that proposed the creation of a new residential system. In his cover letter, Angevine noted that he had not yet received statements from individual committee members, but commented, "I suspect that our differences will not be major ones." Sawyer's copy of the preliminary draft, which became available only in 2012 after the expiration of a fifty-year embargo, showed his extensive editing and many question marks, especially in the sections that described a significant role for "continuing fraternities" following establishment of the new residential system. A compulsive editor, Sawyer habitually marked up documents that came to his desk, but in this instance he had strong reasons to be concerned about the implications of "continuing fraternities." That was the big fault line in the report and in the debates and controversies that followed the release of the report. Bill Gates, a friend and Williams classmate of Sawyer, was very likely acting solely on his own initiative when, in February 1962, he sent the president a copy of his statement on what he thought should be in the committee's final report. Gates had scribbled a note to Sawyer that read, "Jack—this is what I have sent along as my contribution to the Committee."

Gates's statement offered an eloquent educational rationale for removing fraternities, identifying them as a major obstacle to the intellectual vibrancy and educational progress of Williams. He noted that such reforms as total opportunity had largely purged fraternities of the more virulent forms of discrimination. But, he argued, their moral foundation remained a set of values appropriate for a caste organization of the student population rather than values consistent with an inclusive and meritocratic community of learning. The goal of the committee, he concluded, must be the total elimination of fraternities.

He seemed to acknowledge that such was the goal of what he termed the Angevine-Debevoise approach, which he described as "both bold and brilliant." In an effort to understand more fully what Gates meant by the Angevine-Debevoise approach, the author posed the question to Dickinson Debevoise '46 in a conversation on March 29, 2013. Debevoise recalled that he assumed at the time that Gates had referred to the strategy of phasing out fraternities and phasing in the new residential units as smoothly and rapidly as possible, a plan that allowed "continuing fraternities," but with the hope that they would be transitional only, not an ongoing feature of the college.

Gates, who was inclined to the immediate and unconditional elimination of fraternities, worried that the Angevine-Debevoise approach might turn into a major disaster for Williams. A provision for continuing fraternities could serve as a beachhead for them, freed of the encumbrance of total opportunity and more exclusive than ever. Given such an advantage, fraternity proponents might attack, perhaps undermining the new system by claiming that it would be financially unaffordable. Gates was deeply concerned over the risk that the college could regress to a more thoroughly entrenched caste system, undermining the educational gains that had accompanied the fraternity reforms of the previous decade.

To guard against that scenario, Gates insisted that the final report have unanimous or near-unanimous committee support. Even more important, there must be "real teeth" in the committee's report if the Angevine-Debevoise plan were to be adopted. Gates's "teeth" would consist of two conditions. The first was that there must be a fast and aggressive start on organizing the new residential system. The second was a strict timetable to be developed and observed in creating the new system. Adoption of and adherence to those two conditions would help ensure the irreversibility of the new plan.

When the views of Gates are juxtaposed with those of committee member John S. Osborne '25, it is apparent that during the winter of 1962 the Angevine Committee was seriously divided, despite Angevine's assurance to Sawyer that there would be no major differences within it. In Osborne's statement, delivered February 16, 1962, he declared:

I am unwilling to recommend to the Trustees
that they commit for a 100 percent "House" plan
until we have more experience in its operation. I
am likewise unwilling to put the Trustees in the
highly controversial position of abolishing
fraternities until they are given the opportunity to
function in a less important and more natural
environment.

Osborne proposed that the college sponsor what would
be in effect a competition between residential houses and
fraternities. The quota for fraternities would be reduced from 80
percent to 60 percent or less of the student population. The new
residential houses would thus recruit their members from the
remaining 35 or 40 percent. Osborne argued that fraternities were
handicapped because they were compelled to accept members
who were not strongly committed. Many students, he noted,
joined fraternities because that was the only means by which they
could have a social life and decent rooming and dining
opportunities.

The kind of experiment Osborne had in mind would, in
effect, let the market decide what kind of residential and social
organization Williams would eventually have. It is very likely that
this kind of experiment was what Bill Gates had in mind in his
warning of major disasters that could come from missteps by the
committee. Meanwhile, Chairman Angevine had to take seriously
the views of all his committee members. The somewhat vague
"continuing fraternities" language contained in the final report
apparently was the device that achieved the unanimity that Gates
deemed to be essential.

The rapid and firm implementation called for in the
report would help to ensure the irreversibility that Gates also
regarded as imperative. Dick Debevoise, a veteran of the D-Day
landing in Normandy, could be assured that the only direction
the college would move was forward, forward into an uncharted
future, perhaps, aiming to reach the unanimity and equilibrium
that the committee and subsequently the trustees finally achieved.

It would be essential, at least in the end stages, that President Sawyer know the views of various individuals and factions.

Sawyer knew already that the history of fraternities at Williams was replete with ironies and surprises, and he proved himself able to cope with the surprises that he encountered as the committee neared the end of its work. His most surprising moment came when Gates, with the report's final draft in hand, met with him at the President's House shortly before the Angevine Committee delivered it to the trustees. After reading the draft, according to a 1992 interview Sawyer recorded with John Walsh, the president was surprised and concerned by its call for the elimination of the fraternity role "as the focal point for eating, living, and social arrangements" at the college. Sawyer remembered that he said to Gates, in effect, "I think you're out in front of where the students who launched this thing are, and this is going to present some difficulties, perhaps some real difficulties on campus, if they think you've gone farther than they wanted to go." According to Sawyer, Gates replied, "Maybe so, but now it's too late, we have reached our conclusions."

The heart of the Angevine Committee's final report was the recommendation that the college assume responsibility for the housing, dining, and social life of all students in college-owned facilities. The report did not give special emphasis to the shameful record of racial and religious discrimination in the selection of fraternity members, but there was repeated stress on the educational considerations that underlay the committee's recommendations. Indeed, the report defined the purpose of a liberal arts college as providing a "total educational experience" by which students were given "maximum opportunity to make real progress, by constant exposure to diversity and challenge, toward understanding themselves and the world." This educational potential, the committee maintained, could not be realized without the removal of the drag that fraternities were exerting on the institution. By premising the report's recommendations on an educational rationale, the committee was drawing on legal advice offered by Talcott M. Banks '28, the college's attorney. Banks advised that as long as changes were explicitly based upon

101

educational considerations, courts were not likely to challenge those decisions. That legal advice was congruent with the historical fact that, since medieval times, civil authorities had generally respected the autonomy of universities.

The Angevine Report confined fraternities to a nebulous and peripheral role at best, but it did not call for their abolition. As the new residential system developed and the college took over housing and the organization of student social life, the fading fraternities would be left with nothing to do but hold chapter meetings. Still, those who wrote the report had portrayed a future in which fraternities might wish to share facilities if they chose to continue operations within the constraints that the committee had recommended. As we have noted, allowing for the continuation of the greatly weakened fraternities was the price the Angevine Committee paid for unanimous support of its other recommendations. Predictably, however, the suggestion that fraternities might continue as purely fraternal organizations that did not house and feed their members caused considerable confusion and conflict as the college worked its way toward a new residential and social system.

President Sawyer's correspondence and comments in the wake of the release of the Angevine Committee's recommendations revealed that, though almost overwhelmed by the magnitude and complexity of the task ahead of him, he felt a sense of urgency in getting the job done. He could have chosen to slow the timetable and focus on a less radical set of changes. But he had carefully chosen the members of the committee, and now, he concluded, was the time to defer to their judgment. Sawyer said to John Walsh in 1992, "What I'd guessed, and feared...was that...we'd get a badly divided report... ." Sawyer went on to note that he and trustee Mark Cresap '32, who shared his concerns about fraternities, and indeed the board as a whole, "were surprised at the unanimity" with which the committee "came to such far-reaching findings and recommendations."

Embracing those findings and recommendations would not be easy. Shortly before the college released the Angevine Committee report, an obviously worried young president wrote his old mentor, James Phinney Baxter. He confided that implementation of the recommendations was "some months ahead of any timetable I had anticipated, and poses sobering problems affecting the very near future. I would have greatly preferred to have been in office at least a few years before anything of this magnitude came up." The new president and his trustees knew immediately that a tsunami-like torrent of tasks and conflicts awaited them.

"The future of Kappa Alpha at Williams is as obscure to me as it is to you," explained Talcott M. Banks '28, "and so far despite much thought I have been unable to see clearly any form of continuance which appears to have real merit."

However irreversible and inevitable the process of replacing fraternities with a radically new student residential organization may now appear, that was not how it looked in the summer of 1962. When Princeton president Woodrow Wilson (1902-1910) sought a similar transformation of residential life at Princeton as he attempted to integrate its eating clubs into a proposed new residential system, he had the advantage of having been in office for several years. He was able to point to an impressive list of celebrated achievements, and was immensely popular among all the university's constituencies. Even so, his attempt to rein in the eating clubs was a principal factor in the loss of alumni and trustee support that diminished his effectiveness and led him to resign. The odds confronting Sawyer seemed far more formidable than those Wilson faced.

It is reasonable to assume that President Sawyer and the trustees could have bought some time to educate the alumni and the on-campus community before setting out on the long, difficult journey that the Angevine Committee advocated. Indeed, Bill Gates had devised a back-up plan that very likely would have served that purpose well. He outlined that plan in a communication with President Sawyer during the crucial weeks when the Angevine committee was trying to shape and agree upon a final report to the trustees.

Gates's alternative plan would have fallen short of eliminating fraternities, as he himself favored, but it would have met and exceeded the demands of the student petitioners. His reasoning seemed to be that if the Angevine Committee or the trustees should prove to be irresolute regarding the scope of the changes to the fraternity system, the reforms of the past decade would stand a better chance of surviving as a platform for further evolution if the college stayed on the incremental reform path. The steps that Gates had in mind included a total opportunity process wherein all fraternities shared equal responsibility for its success; banning of the blackball and all other veto devices in the selection of fraternity members; the elimination of all vestiges of hazing and discrimination from the life of the college; and a plan whereby the college would assume responsibility for the taxes, insurance, and maintenance expenses of any fraternity houses whose trustees would turn over title to those properties to the college and agree that they would henceforth operate as clubs rather than as fraternities.

Many of the fraternities had deferred maintenance worries and budget concerns and at least some doubtless would have welcomed a college offer to take over title to their properties and assume the attendant financial obligations. In brief, under the Gates plan, President Sawyer and the trustees could have diminished the fraternity presence gradually rather than hustling them towards the exit door immediately.

Sawyer's conflicting instincts about whether to proceed with the fraternity issue as rapidly as the Angevine Committee proposed or at a slower and more deliberate pace were reflected in the deliberations of the trustees as well during the period between May and December 1962. The minutes of their meetings reveal wide divisions within the board on that question. President Sawyer had to listen to all those voices, while recognizing that his views would likely be determinative. The Angevine Committee wanted to move on a fast track. Past study committees, however, had set a precedent for approaching fraternity issues in incremental steps, and it was Sawyer's own nature to approach change cautiously and carefully. Echoing the sentiment that he had expressed in his letter to President Baxter regarding the Angevine Committee recommendations, he often remarked in other correspondence that he would have preferred a more deliberate timetable for the changes that were undertaken.

Frederick Rudolph '42, commenting upon undergraduates who sought fraternity reforms: "Of course they need watching, but even more, they need to be joined, assisted, and given the benefit of conscious creative direction."

Long after the fraternity battle was over, Anne Sawyer reported that her husband sometimes mused that perhaps there would have been less conflict and acrimony had the process been more extended. Late in his life, Sawyer suggested that perhaps he had behaved "innocently" by readily agreeing to trustee Mark Cresap's offer to provide leadership in persuading the board to abolish fraternities if Sawyer would undertake the administrative responsibility for implementing the decision. Yet, in the end, Sawyer overcame his doubts and committed himself to the process and the timetable indicated by the Angevine Committee. He and the trustees chose to face into the storm and fully implement the committee's recommendations as rapidly as possible.

By following the lead of the Angevine Committee, Sawyer, whether or not he recognized it explicitly, demonstrated that his dominant instinct was to keep faith with the student petitioners and other reform advocates. As Professor Fred Rudolph had written in an article for the July 1961 issue of the *Alumni Review*, which appeared just as President Sawyer was assuming his new duties, thanks to the initiatives of students, "the reforms are already underway. The problem is to give shape and direction to what is now only the uninvited, uncontrolled, impact of a generation of young students perhaps more promising and more creative than any the college has ever known. Like the generations before them, they are the reformers. Of course they need watching, but even more, they need to be joined, assisted, and given the benefit of conscious creative direction."

In teaming up with Grinnell and his reform-minded colleagues in the summer of 1961, and then again in backing unreservedly the far-reaching recommendations of the Angevine Committee in 1962, Sawyer was providing the "conscious, creative direction"—in short, the leadership—that Rudolph was urging and that Sawyer himself instinctively saw as his role.

That leadership would be severely tested in the struggle to bring the college's two largest stakeholder groups, the alumni and the students, over to the cause of transforming change. The first big task was to educate them in the realities of a deeply dysfunctional residential and social system, the second to create a structure that was compatible with the college's educational character and goals.

The campaign to win the support of alumni and students got off to a bad start when the Angevine Report was publicly released abruptly on June 30, 1962. Acrimony and conflict erupted when it became known that an interval of almost two months had passed between the trustees' receipt of the report on May 5 and its public release. The final faculty meeting of the year, commencement, and reunions had come and gone with no mention of the revolutionary changes that were impending. That delay later led to accusations that the trustees and the administration had attempted a sneak attack on fraternities. A less sinister and more obvious explanation, as indicated earlier, was that the president and trustees were simply unprepared for the recommendations of the Angevine Committee's report and needed time to think through how they were going to respond.

Still, it is easy to understand why the pattern of communications appeared less than transparent. In a three-page memorandum dated June 18, 1962, and addressed to undergraduates, the college had announced a number of initiatives and decisions, including that compulsory chapel had been abolished. Buried in the middle of the memorandum was a five-line paragraph that noted that the Angevine Committee had submitted its report and that copies of it would be mailed to students, alumni, and faculty in the near future. Its recommendations, the announcement concluded, "will deserve thoughtful consideration."

Indeed, the *New York Times* appeared to have better access to the thinking of the college administration than the Williams community had. On July 2, 1962, the *Times* carried a story that reported trustee receipt of the Angevine recommendations just as mailed copies of the report were arriving at the addresses of members of the various Williams constituencies. Appearing without a byline, the *Times* article emphasized that, although fraternities would be permitted to continue, the widespread view was that without the income from rooming and dining charges, it would be economically impossible for them to survive. The telling of the story suggested that it had emanated from the Williams administration. Although Ralph Renzi '42, the Williams news director at that time, could not recall a half-century later exactly how the article had come about, he acknowledged the likelihood that he had a large role in producing it. If so, he almost certainly worked with Sawyer at his shoulder, since the president habitually took a direct role in shaping news releases that dealt with delicate and important issues.

Unfortunately, the various communications emanating from Williams regarding fraternity matters hardly presented a clear and coherent story. The boldness suggested by the *Times* story was at odds with the cautious tone of the trustee statement of June 30, 1962. The board statement concurred with the Angevine Committee's conclusion that fraternities as they once were had ceased to exist at Williams, and agreed with the committee's analysis "of the history and long-term evolution of the fraternity system" and "that provision of housing, eating, and social accommodations is properly a responsibility of the college." The statement did not, however, assert that the board would act on the report's recommendations. Instead, it stressed the importance of avoiding hasty and arbitrary responses "in an area of long history and deep attachments." The statement urged that fraternities "review their relation to the college in the light of the Committee Report. The Board wishes to invite initiative on the part of the several fraternities and to remain responsive to conditions and circumstances as they may develop voluntarily or through negotiation."

Many read the statement as an invitation from the trustees for the fraternities to join them at the negotiating table, interpreting the committee report as an opening ploy in a negotiating process. In any event, the trustee statement that accompanied the release of the Angevine Committee report on June 30, 1962, was an important part of a pattern of puzzlingly slow, hesitating, and ambiguous official responses to the Angevine Committee's call for rapid, decisive action.

PART III
BUILDING A LEARNING CULTURE
FOR GLOBAL CITIZENSHIP

ALPHA DELTA PHI JAMBOREE, CA. 1957

Chapter 6.
The Standing Committee
Creates the Future
1962-1970

In October 1962, President Sawyer and the trustees finally declared clearly and categorically their readiness to implement fully the epochal recommendations of the Angevine Committee report. There would be no delay or reconsideration. They bared their teeth as Bill Gates had urged them to do. But reaching that point had been a gradual process.

The first meetings of the trustees after the release of Angevine Report was held on June 8-10, 1962. A third day had been added to the session in recognition of the report's revolutionary importance. As the trustees delved into the implications of what the committee had proposed and started to appreciate the magnitude and complexity of what lay ahead of them, they spent all three days discussing the report and how to respond to it publicly.

Trustee Mark Cresap, CEO of the Westinghouse Corporation was especially close to Sawyer. He was unable to attend the June 1962 sessions because of health problems that would lead to his death a year later. However, he communicated his strong view that the trustees should face the fraternity problem with decisive and unhesitating action. For Cresap, that meant board approval and full implementation of the committee's recommendations. Not all his fellow trustees, however, rushed to his corner.

Some openly voiced their disagreement with the report. The majority expressed apprehension about the likely alienation of large numbers of alumni and students. A prominent theme in the conversation was the need to proceed cautiously and slowly. Trustee John Osborne had some company in advocating that the college test the report's central recommendation by creating and evaluating one or two model student residential units.

Almost everyone agreed upon the urgent need to educate the alumni to the coming changes, whatever they might be. Anticipating widespread alumni alienation, trustee Bernard Auer '39 suggested engagement of public relations counsel to advise the board. As Sawyer reported many years later, the trustees and faculty were so close to the serious problems presented by fraternities that they failed to appreciate how uninformed the alumni were. Consistent with the stands he would soon take as chair of the Standing Committee, trustee Talcott (Ted) Banks '28 warned against delays, arguing that they would further divide the larger Williams community. Had he been there to hear that appeal, Bill Gates would have been reassured.

Though the trustees reached no final decision on the Angevine recommendations at their June meeting, they launched an education campaign beginning with the release of the report to the public at the end of June and the appointment in July of a Standing Committee. The new committee's main task would be implementation of changes in the college's residential system, but it would also perform an important educational function. Ted Banks, the committee chair, was a senior partner of Palmer and Dodge, a prominent Boston law firm, who also brought extensive experience as board chair of both the Boston Symphony Orchestra and the Clark Art Institute. He had joined the Williams board just as Jack Sawyer became president.

Banks did not wait for marching orders from his fellow trustees. Almost immediately, he and his committee colleagues went to work explaining the meaning of the Angevine Committee recommendations to such groups as the Gargoyle Alumni Association, undergraduate Gargoyle members, the Junior Advisers, College Council officers, and editors of the *Williams Record*. Expressions of support soon began to come in from those groups. The committee kept the momentum going by identifying the subcommittees that would develop various components of the new residential organization. More than one hundred fifty students applied for the forty places reserved for undergraduates on those subcommittees. Banks and his committee colleagues initiated discussions with the officers of alumni fraternity corporations about transferring ownership of their houses to the college.

The leadership of Banks and the work of the Standing Committee during the summer and early autumn of 1962 had a catalyzing effect on the board of trustees when it met in October. The earlier statements of the board had been tentative enough to encourage the view that they were testing the sentiments among the various Williams constituencies, but the time had come to remove all doubt about the inclinations of the president and trustees. Upon the strong recommendation of the Standing Committee, the trustees issued an unequivocal declaration of commitment to the Angevine Committee recommendations on October 6, 1962. At the close of the two-day meeting of the board, the trustee issued this statement:

> After long consideration the Board has voted that
> the policy of the College is to provide housing,
> eating, and social accommodations for the entire
> student body, and to authorize the Standing
> Committee to continue negotiations with
> fraternities and others and to proceed with plans
> for the provision of residential units, one or more
> of which should be available by the beginning of
> the next academic year.

No one knew how long it would take to accomplish the daunting task that that the Standing Committee had undertaken. In language heard frequently during World War II, the members of the new committee understood that they had signed on "for the duration." In fact, approximately six years would pass before the Standing Committee, near the end of 1968, had won strong enough support for the recommended changes and was close enough to having completed the transition to a new residential and social system that the remaining steps could be left to college officers.

In addition to Banks, the Standing Committee included Dickinson Debevoise '46, veteran of both the Sterling and

113

Angevine committees; Williams Treasurer Charles Foehl '32; and two faculty members, history professor Fred Rudolph '42 and art professor Whitney Stoddard '35. J. Hodge Markgraf '52 of the chemistry department was named secretary of the Standing Committee, having served in the same role for the Angevine Committee. The committee's staff assistant, and later an assistant dean, was Donald W. Gardner, Jr. '57, a member of St. Anthony who, as a student, had been a leading member of the Committee of 22, the group that had advocated the total elimination of fraternities. Although not a formal member of the Standing Committee, Alfred E. (Jake) Driscoll '25 was a valuable contributor to its work, especially in negotiations regarding the transfer of fraternity properties to the college. Driscoll, a trustee, was the CEO of Warner-Lambert Pharmaceutical Co., and a former governor of New Jersey.

Whereas the Angevine Committee necessarily deliberated in secrecy once it concluded its hearings, the work of the Standing Committee eventually involved the participation of scores of students, faculty, staff, and alumni. The Standing Committee assigned the work of envisioning and planning the future residential system to five subcommittees: Student Government, Social Activities, Cultural Activities and Athletics, Physical Facilities, and Procedures for Student Choice of Social Units and Freshman Inclusion. Membership of the subcommittees included more than three dozen undergraduates. Benjamin Labaree, dean of the college, and John Hyde, as dean of freshmen and later as Labaree's successor, were actively involved with all five subcommittees, as was Donald (Dee) Gardner. Fred Rudolph and Bill Pierson, faculty representatives on the Standing Committee, were heavily invested in designing the system of faculty fellows and alumni associates who would be affiliated with the houses, and gathering suggestions of people who would be effective in those roles.

In responding to the overwhelming volume of correspondence and calls, communicating with regional alumni groups and alumni fraternity corporations, and supplying information essential to planning the new residential and social system, the Standing Committee routinely turned for assistance to Development Director Willard Dickerson '40, Alumni Relations Director John English '32, and Provost Joseph Kershaw. Professors Benjamin W. Labaree and John M. Hyde '52 sat regularly with the committee and contributed significantly to shaping the new residential system. Labaree was dean of the college from 1963 to 1967. As Hyde would put it a half century later, the Standing Committee envisioned the new residential houses as "fraternities without rushing." That was a logical starting point for the new era that ensued with the disappearance of fraternities.

A member of Saint Anthony fraternity, Donald Gardner '57 became a leading member of the most radical student reform movement, the Committee of 22, which demanded the total elimination of fraternities five years before the trustee action of 1962.

Staff assistant Donald Gardner, only a few years older than the undergraduates, served as the committee's eyes and ears as he interacted with student fraternity members. He tried to get a handle on the probabilities of resistance and cooperation in response to the college's efforts to persuade fraternities to turn over their houses for integration into the new residential system. It was not surprising that undergraduate fraternity members viewed Gardner as a kind of espionage agent in their midst. He became a favorite scapegoat who received much verbal abuse, and not always with cheerful forbearance. His boss, Ted Banks, an avid sailor who loved his time aboard his boat *Spar Hawk* counseled his young assistant that it was wise to ignore small eddies and pay attention to the larger tides.

115

Banks's was wise advice, since Williams was facing seas as choppy as any it had known in its long history. During the late summer of 1962, as the alumni body woke up to what had happened and what they feared was about to happen, aggrieved alumni began to organize efforts to block and reverse trustee efforts to carry out the report's recommendations. As for the students, when they arrived back on campus in September they mounted ugly demonstrations in front of the President's House that featured derisive chants. Buildings and Grounds workers stayed busy removing insulting messages to Sawyer painted on the white exterior of the President's House, among them "Hit the road, Jack." Michael Katz '66 remembered bonfires in front of Chapin Hall where effigies of Sawyer were lowered into the flames accompanied by chants of "Turkey! Turkey!"

With approximately 80 percent of undergraduate fraternity members having declared their opposition to the Angevine recommendations, President Sawyer, in concert with Banks, moved quickly and quietly to line up support among student leaders, starting almost as soon as they returned to campus in September 1962. Sawyer met with the College Council, editors of the *Williams Record*, and Gargoyle. Soon there were formal expressions of support from those groups. *Record* editorials consistently endorsed the college's new plans for the future.

Alumni leaders were not so easily won over. Organized opposition to the Angevine recommendations began in July. Just as Sawyer had anticipated, and even as the Standing Committee was organizing to begin its monumental task, disgruntled alumni launched a fierce counterattack designed to reverse or delay implementation of the proposed changes and to discourage fraternity corporations from turning over their houses to the college. The most aggressive and widespread effort came from the Williams Alumni Action Committee (WAAC), an ad hoc body established soon after the release of the Angevine Committee report, which called for boycotts of the Alumni Fund, withholding other forms of financial support, and refusal to turn fraternity residences over to the college. Hostile and noisy scenes at some regional alumni meetings were similar in some ways to the on-campus demonstrations by students against President Sawyer.

From numerous alumni sources came strong appeals for a moratorium on implementation of the report for at least a year and perhaps two or three years. During that interval there could be further study of the issues, the argument went, along with better education of the alumni and perhaps a referendum among them. Some proposed, as had been discussed within the Angevine Committee and among the trustees, that a competition be conducted between the fraternities and a demonstration model of the proposed new residential system. Standing Committee chairman Ted Banks firmly rejected all suggestions for delay, making himself a lightning rod for infuriated alumni.

There was honest confusion and doubt among alumni fueled by what they saw as conflicting messages within the text of the report itself and, especially, among those who spoke as advocates for the proposed changes. Some alumni and students claimed that the report cited very little evidence to justify the dramatic diminution or disappearance of the historic role of fraternities, and some trustees acknowledged that the report was thin on evidence. Many doubted the report's assurances that fraternities might continue as "truly fraternal" organizations that would not be permitted to feed or house their members or organize their social life. The report suggested that fraternities that wished to continue might jointly arrange for spaces that would accommodate their reduced activities. As late as early 1963, trustee Henry N. Flynt, as chair of the board's executive committee, spoke of the possibility of using one or two off-campus spaces for fraternity meetings and even social events that were purely fraternal. Yet Ted Banks repeatedly stated that he could not conceive of any circumstances under which fraternities could survive financially or be compatible with the new residential system that his committee was charged with creating.

Banks's resolute stand against encouraging any initiative to perpetuate fraternity activity provoked his Kappa Alpha fraternity brother, Henry W. (Hank) Comstock '25, to accuse him of using every means to extirpate the fraternity presence at

Williams. Comstock exploded, "In short, I am thoroughly disgusted with your lack of sincerity." He argued that Banks, instead of trying to banish fraternities entirely, should be offering encouragement "to those of us who don't want to scuttle the traditions of over one hundred years." Comstock commended what he described as the contrasting attitude of Angevine Committee member John Osborne '25, citing a letter in which Osborne wrote that at a recent KA meeting in Williamstown, "the subject of keeping the Kap Society on the Williams campus was discussed...[and] it was the unanimous sentiment of all...that a committee should be organized to see how our desires can best be carried out."

The confusion and conflict about continuing fraternities was not the only focal point of alumni and student skepticism and questioning. Underlying the entire matter was the fundamental question of what the real fraternity problem was. The central argument of the Angevine Committee was, as reformers had argued for decades, that the fraternity culture clashed with the college's educational mission. Fraternities were a liability that kept the college from realizing its full potential as a learning institution. The fraternity enclaves discouraged the kind of campus-wide deep dialogue and friendships that would enable students to learn from each other. As the committee saw it, the rushing process, initiation rites, and other activities consumed an inordinate amount of student time that might otherwise have been applied to academic tasks. The atmosphere within fraternity houses was widely viewed as disruptive to academic work. Contributing factors to that unfavorable environment that were often cited included the presence of women at unauthorized times, consumption of alcoholic beverages, and partying during the more academically demanding parts of the week.

Members of pre-World War I classes were dismayed by such reports. They remembered fraternity houses where women and alcohol were both banned, and their parties routinely included chaperones. They tended to view the changes in behavioral norms as a sign of breakdown in moral standards. The two themes of immoral behavior and conditions that disrupted academic work could not be clearly separated, and it is not surprising that some advocates for the changes recommended in the Angevine Committee report dwelt principally on one theme and others emphasized both.

In response to the concerns of Harry Biggins '11 about questionable moral behavior, Jay Angevine downplayed it as a "side issue."

"No one has said that the houses are 'dens of infamy,' regardless of how you may view the panorama from the bar-rooms to the locked bedrooms. ... [T]he problem is not that, but rather whether the college is under present conditions doing as well as it can the job entrusted to it."

Yet that was not how it appeared to many alumni. It is understandable that attention would be drawn to what was seen as reprehensible behavior; those conditions were easy to picture. The educational rationale for the proposed changes, however, was more difficult to explain and comprehend. Furthermore, alumni concern over behavior in the fraternities was stimulated by continuing attention to that theme in what some representatives of the college reported to alumni. In alumni gatherings on campus and across the country, President Sawyer himself frequently dwelt upon serious behavior problems in the fraternities. During Sawyer's first presidential year three students died in automobile accidents where alcohol played a role, and automobile accidents resulting in serious student injuries were not uncommon. As indicated by his speeches and correspondence, Sawyer was distressed by this evidence that some fraternities had become, in effect, driving-and-drinking clubs.

Older alumni tended to view reports of alcohol abuse and sexual misbehavior as indications that Williams was admitting applicants with questionable backgrounds and values. Others asked why the college administration did not crack down more severely on such conduct. In a letter to Banks, his classmate Donald Edgar '28 described the information and impressions he picked up from a campus visit: "If conditions are as bad as President Sawyer described that evening—immorality, obscenity, drunkenness, untruthfulness, passive resistance, imposed mediocrity, etc.—I must conclude that there has been a complete breakdown in campus discipline. Is there no Dean? Has no one the courage to deal with individual miscreants?" Others suggested that the apparently lax behavioral standards indicated that Williams was appointing faculty members who did not appreciate the traditions of the college. Some correspondents suggested that what they perceived as an egalitarian hostility to fraternities was driven by a Communist mentality that had infected the campus.

Then there were those who were skeptical about Williams' ability to improve undergraduate behavior by simply housing students in college-owned buildings. John Kifner '63, editor of the *Williams Record*, spoke for many students when he observed that, if the Angevine Committee was principally concerned about sin, he had seen as much of it in the dormitories as in the fraternities. Although school heads as a group were almost unanimous in applauding the changes stemming from the Angevine Committee's recommendations, some reactions were more nuanced. In a letter to Ted Banks, Paul Wright '27, the highly respected head of Groton School, expressed strong support for the college's new plans. He disagreed, however, with the emphasis on curbing questionable student behavior. He expressed doubt that contemporary fraternity members' moral behavior was much different from that of fraternity men in his own time as a student. The educational reasons for the changes, he argued, should be the emphasis.

With reformers describing questionable student behavior as an important aspect of the fraternity problem, many alumni worried that the new residential system would entail a larger *in loco parentis* role for the college similar to that of many prep schools. As Donald Edgar put it, "I hope the campus does not become too like Vassar nor (sic) a church prep school."

In noting the widespread confusion and distress among older alumni following release of the Angevine Report, it is important to understand that unhappiness was hardly less pronounced among recent graduates. Whereas older alumni stressed the fraternities that they had known and loved decades earlier, recent graduates were more attentive to the text of the report itself. Many found it lacking in evidence and information, ambiguous, and vague. A common complaint was that the report offered few clues about what the future residential system would look like. If the Angevine Report had been a class exercise, they would have given it a low grade. While the report was a politically brilliant document, it was less successful as a cogent and convincing argument for change.

Recent graduates and current students who found themselves unsatisfied with the explanation for the proposed new directions included young men who would become major scholars or nationally prominent in their careers, as well as future trustees and some who would prove among the largest donors in Williams' history. The internal struggles among members of the larger alumni family should not be viewed as a contest between the children of light and the children of darkness. The vast majority of the participants were honest, honorable, civil, and genuinely distressed over disagreements with classmates and fellow alumni.

What are we to make of the claims that the Angevine Committee's report was vague, lacking in evidence, and ambiguous? In assessing those charges it is well to remember that the goal was to produce a report that had the approval of all or virtually all Angevine Committee members and then all or an overwhelming majority of the trustees. Although the Angevine Committee was badly split over precisely what should be in the final report, as was the board of trustees, reaching a larger consensus was deemed to be essential to implementation of the report's recommendations and the long-term health and cohesion of the college. One result of that compromise process was the lack of specificity in the report's prescriptions.

Most contentious and confusing of all was the allowance for continuing fraternities. The internal dynamics of the committee and of the board of trustees resulted in a report and set of recommendations whose genius was primarily political, not analytical. An additional consideration that made for a political document was the desire to emerge from the controversy with as little damage to the college's reputation as possible. A more candid and detailed case against fraternities for the recommended changes in the college's organization of residential life would have resulted in hanging out for public view much of the college's historical dirty laundry, particularly that of racial and religious discrimination. Another disadvantage in a too-detailed case against fraternities was the risk of prolonging the controversy. These considerations have led this observer to conclude that while the critics' claims had considerable merit, President Sawyer and the trustees showed great practical wisdom and political skill in achieving the goal of replacing an outmoded residential system with one that greatly enhanced the college's educational stature and reputation.

Although the trustees tried to protect President Sawyer from the worst of the turmoil, his leadership role in the crisis put him at the center of the storm. Anne Sawyer remembered that it was especially difficult for him to deal with the grievances of older alumni. Many of them had been friends of his father, William Sawyer '08, who had died at the relatively young age of fifty-eight. The future Williams president had first met many of those who were now angry and upset at him when, as a young boy, he accompanied his father to Williams events. President Sawyer did not like conflict, and sometimes literally became ill in the face of it, as when he fainted during a tense meeting of Los Angeles alumni.

When Sawyer realized that there was no going back—he reached the same conclusion that Debevoise had during the Angevine Committee's deliberations—he plunged into initiatives designed to educate alumni on the issues and his plans for the educational progress of Williams. Throughout the controversy over the Angevine Report, President Sawyer repeatedly acknowledged that Williams had not done a good job of educating and communicating with its alumni about the college's leading issues and larger trends. The trustees encouraged Sawyer in his efforts to remedy that failing. A key part of his strategy became to get opinion leaders into his corner, confident that the constituencies they represented would tend to line up behind them. He worked to enlist support among influential alumni, such as Francis B. Sayre '37, dean of the Washington Cathedral.

A prominent component of the college's alumni education effort was the Williams Today program, launched in October 1962. It brought groups of alumni and their spouses to the campus for long weekends, where they heard presentations and engaged in discussions that included Sawyer, numerous faculty members, and administrative officers. Those programs proved to be highly effective. They did not emphasize the fraternity conflict but looked to the future, a future that would include a new residential system, new curricular directions, a larger college, enhanced financial resources, and possibly women students. There was also great interest in the college's recent purchase of Mount Hope Farm and how it might figure in Williams' future development.

Alumni responded very positively to the increased access to faculty members and principal college administrative officers. They were more accustomed to alumni events that featured talks by Coach Len Watters about the latest football victory over Amherst or prospects for the coming season. Watters had been an effective ambassador, but alumni welcomed a broader and deeper exposure that reached into the college's basic educational mission and programs and how the president viewed the future.

Sawyer mapped out his vision for the college as a learning institution in a report titled Plans and Purposes, which appeared in May 1963 and was very favorably received. One of Sawyer's frustrations as a trustee had been the lack of movement toward reforming a curriculum whose basic structure had been frozen for fifty years; as president, he could make that goal his own. The Plans and Purposes document and the discussions that occurred during the Williams Today sessions and on other occasions revealed the president to be an educational leader with fresh ideas regarding the curriculum.

As Sawyer and his colleagues explained the educational context into which the new residential system would fit, phasing out the traditional fraternities made sense to increasing numbers of alumni and students. The members of the Student Curriculum

Committee were kept apprised of Sawyer's thinking and the work of the various faculty committees that were studying curricular proposals. Students and alumni were excited by proposed plans to add such fields as anthropology, sociology, and environmental studies to the curriculum. Both groups responded positively to the possibility of reducing the student course load from five per semester to four so as to allow for greater depth of exploration. Similarly, they were attracted by the prospect of making the curriculum more flexible and richer by offering fewer year-long courses, many of which stretched out unnecessarily, and greatly increasing the number of semester-length courses.

Alumni listened approvingly to the president's description of an Area Studies program that would greatly expand curricular attention to Asia, Latin America, Africa, and the Middle East. They heard him describe the need for a new science facility, later fulfilled in the form of the Bronfman Science Center, which would be responsive to trends that were making more permeable the disciplinary walls and resulting in such new specialties as biophysics, physical chemistry, and biochemistry. They learned of Sawyer's thoughts about a graduate program in art history that would utilize the impressive resources of the Clark Art Institute. Students were pleased when Williams added Russian to its list of courses, and there was campus-wide interest in the college's plans to install audio-visual instructional technology when Phi Delta Theta was converted to the Weston Language Center.

On the other side of the fraternity battle line, the Williams Alumni Action Committee in a newsletter that appeared on June 7, 1963, ten days following the release of Plans and Purposes, complained that students were "beginning to believe in the inevitability of the proposed system." The WAAC statement was recognition that President Sawyer's hard work and imaginative arguments were having the desired effect. A growing majority in the larger Williams community had accepted the need for change, a belief that he buttressed with concrete achievements and exciting plans.

Even as Sawyer and his colleagues were preparing alumni for the birth of a new Williams, two members of the Angevine Committee, John Osborne, and especially Jay Angevine himself, reminded alumni that the action of the trustees in redefining responsibility for the housing, dining, and social life of students did not preclude the continuation of fraternities. Angevine, for a brief period in the autumn of 1962, devoted himself to spelling out his vision of those continuing fraternities, driven perhaps by a combination of personal convictions on the subject and by feelings of obligation to keep faith with trustee and committee colleagues who had reluctantly agreed to the Angevine Committee's recommendations.

In an October 19, 1962, letter to his Williams contemporary Ted Thurston '12, written soon after the Standing Committee had begun its work, Angevine stated, "If fraternities can reclaim their former virtue, more power to them. We never recommended that they be abolished." In his speech earlier that month to the Alumni Fund class agents at their annual campaign kick-off dinner, Angevine had gone further, staking a claim for fraternities of the future that "would...be subject to overall college policies but would be free of present economic pressure to put elections on an assembly line basis that contradicts the concept on which fraternities are based. There are many fraternal organizations that achieve distinction without any dependence on bed and board."

That future, as Angevine saw it, would mean the elimination of the mechanistic approach of total opportunity and a return to the past when fraternity members chose new members strictly on the basis of their own preferences. As unrealistic as that view might seem today, and however fraught it was with the dangers that Bill Gates perceived, one can understand the appeal it held for older alumni fifty years ago, whose memories of fraternities were overwhelmingly favorable.

Angevine's vision looked to the past again when he recalled that in the first several decades of fraternities at Williams, they typically had a meeting room in a dormitory or other building while their members lived and dined with students from other fraternities. He noted that the grand fraternity houses came later.

Like the church reformers of the late Medieval and early Renaissance period, Angevine seemed to envision a leap backward to what he viewed as the simplicity and purity of an earlier era. The fact that the Angevine Committee report made scant mention of the history of racial and religious discrimination in the fraternity bidding process perhaps obscured for the moment the lack of realism in the vision of the future fraternity as a repristination of the pre-modern fraternity.

Standing Committee chairman Ted Banks understood clearly the problem with Angevine's view of the future. While we are aware of no communication between them on the subject, oral or written, Banks left ample evidence of his view that fraternities had no legitimate future at Williams, and he felt no obligation to try to respond to alumni appeals for guidance on the kinds of fraternity activities that would be permitted. Whether intended or accidental, the virtually antiphonal themes emanating from Angevine and Banks both contributed importantly to the progress of the Standing Committee: Angevine kept the dialogue going with older alumni, while Banks held firmly to the strategy of complete elimination of the fraternity system even as he strove to build the new order.

In the summer of 1962, Banks's own fraternity, Kappa Alpha, became the first to announce that it was ready to cooperate by turning its house and land over to the college to be used in establishing the new system. The momentum that led to that decision came largely from the support of James Phinney Baxter, Sawyer's predecessor and a KA alumnus, and the leadership of James Blume '63, who was president of KA and also of the Interfraternity Council.

Kappa Alpha's announcement of its intention to cooperate with the college was touted as a good example for other fraternities. Still, as John Osborne's letter to Henry Comstock attested, there was strong interest within the KA ranks in maintaining a campus presence, and that sentiment led to the decision to reserve some land as a site for a possible new and presumably more modest building. Banks and others were apprehensive that Kappa Alpha could end up setting a troublesome precedent by investing time, energy, and money in building, buying, or leasing a new fraternity house. In a letter to Huntington Gilchrist '13 on October 18, 1963, Banks stated, "The future of Kappa Alpha at Williams is as obscure to me as it is to you, and so far despite much thought I have been unable to see clearly any form of continuance which appears to have real merit."

Against this background of conflict over continuing fraternities, Banks wrote a memorandum on November 14 for the benefit of his committee colleagues. This document is revealing of Banks's humanity and wisdom and also of his political realism and his determination to stay the course in carrying out the mandate to create a new residential system that evidently would completely replace fraternities. The memorandum appeared to be largely in response to a letter a month earlier, on October 17, 1963, from Ted Thurston '12, in which Thurston explained that older alumni were having a difficult time understanding and accepting the action of the trustees. He appealed for forbearance, tact, and understanding in the Standing Committee's dealings with older alumni. Using language very similar to Thurston's, Banks called upon his committee colleagues to be gentle and empathetic in communicating with older alumni who were reluctant to accept the new program.

Still, Banks would yield no ground on what he believed to be the crucial issue for the Standing Committee. He argued that any proposal for a continuing fraternity must clearly and explicitly spell out the conditions that would apply. The burden of proof lay with the petitioning fraternity, not with the college. There must be reliable and enforceable assurances that the purposes of a continuing fraternity would be in full accord with the policy of the college's new house system. In addition, a continuing fraternity would have to have an alumni organization that would provide ongoing supervision. In effect, Banks set the bar high enough that it was doubtful any proposed continuing fraternity could clear it.

The bottom line for Banks was that members of the Standing Committee, though showing respect, compassion, and patience, should provide alumni no encouragement concerning a future for fraternities. Implicitly acknowledging that some of the language of the Angevine Committee report was ambiguous and unclear, Banks made the interesting point that the lack of clarity made the report more palatable to older alumni who were deeply attached to their fraternities. Readers had latitude in interpreting its meaning, but the job of the Standing Committee, as Banks saw it, was to remain resolute and let time become its crucial ally, as individual fraternities gradually became aligned with the new program and graduating fraternity devotees were replaced by students who had not participated in the old culture and history.

The elimination of fraternities constituted just half the battle; the Standing Committee also had the mammoth task of shaping a new residential system. At the outset, alumni and student skeptics had a virtually blank canvas on which to project their doubts and fears; on the other side of the discussion, the Standing Committee had its own blank canvas.

Committee members looked around for possible models and found none that suited Williams entirely. They looked at Harvard and Yale, making a thorough inspection of Ezra Stiles College at Yale as guests of its master, Richard Sewall '32. While observing that Harvard and Yale were admirably served by their residential systems, and that their arrangements might provide some lessons for Williams, the committee concluded that Williams had neither the money nor the need to match the house and college systems with their infrastructure of faculty tutors, libraries, athletic facilities, and separate dining halls. Whereas a Yale college typically had a membership of approximately 450 students, the Standing Committee was envisioning residential houses that provided for sixty to ninety students.

An inspection of plans for Bowdoin's senior center (later named the Coles Tower) led to the quick verdict that it was not the right model for Williams. Dean of the College Robert R. R.

Brooks, who had attended Oxford as a Rhodes Scholar, advised that the Oxford colleges were too large to provide useful lessons for Williams.

After looking afar for lessons and models that could usefully inform the planning for a new residential system, attention turned to what could be created from the existing housing stock and dining facilities of the old fraternity houses and dormitories. Fortunately, the new Prospect House had just come into use in 1962 to accommodate a modest enrollment expansion planned by President Baxter. The trustees quickly authorized the construction of a new dining hall (later named Driscoll Hall) adjacent to Prospect. The college's plans for the future residential system came to include the Williams Inn as the lease by the Treadway Corporation approached expiration.

The negotiations with the fifteen fraternity corporations for transfer of their houses stretched out until 1972, when St. Anthony, after years of discussion, turned its house over to the college to be used by the Center for Development Economics for the housing, feeding, and classroom instruction of its students. Most fraternities that agreed to have their houses become part of the new residential system proceeded initially on the basis of three-year leases, and some fraternities continued to use the houses even as they were being incorporated into the new organization. The result was an uncertain schedule for the transition, although the momentum into the future gathered speed through the years. The process effectively concluded only after the graduation of the class of 1970, after which, by trustee edict, no further fraternity activity was permitted.

Of the fifteen fraternity houses on the campus when Sawyer arrived as president in 1961, ten would eventually provide housing for undergraduates under the new residential system. In some cases two or even three of the old structures were combined into a single residential unit because of the general aim to keep the number of students in a unit in the range of sixty to ninety men. Most of the repurposed fraternity houses were renamed for historically prominent members of the fraternities.

Several fraternities made clear early in the negotiations that they would transfer their houses only on condition that they would be used for purposes other than housing undergraduates. Another complication was posed by Sawyer's conviction that Williams needed to increase the number of students significantly in order to realize economies of scale and to make possible the introduction of new fields of study. These circumstances pointed to the need to build at least one new housing and dining complex. An interesting historical irony also entered the picture when it became evident that that the most logical site for the needed buildings was the Greylock Hotel property, purchased by the trustees in 1937, the deal that had led to President Dennett's resignation.

The emerging Greylock complex would play a pivotal role in the creation of the new order. Planning for it began in 1962 as the Standing Committee was starting its work. Jack Sawyer, who often said that had he not become an academic he would probably have been an architect, was intimately involved in Greylock's creation, taking a direct interest in the choice of architects and design decisions. Sawyer recognized the importance of the project in winning acceptance of the new residential alternative to fraternities. As he later wrote, he also recognized "the urgency of pouring concrete for new foundations to make clear to any doubters that the new policies of the College were now firmly in place."

The chosen architect, Ben Thompson of the Architects Collaborative (TAC) of Cambridge, Massachusetts, caught Sawyer's spirit and entered enthusiastically into the Greylock project. Some of the features that figured in the early discussion of Greylock, which included an adjacent branch of the central library, guest suites for house officers and distinguished visitors, special study areas and reference collections for the four residential houses in the complex, were abandoned as too costly and unnecessary. But as Thompson produced drawings and models of the new complex, and as the ground for the large project was prepared, the on-campus Williams community and the alumni glimpsed a compelling picture of the future. With growing enthusiasm, they realized that a new Williams was well on its way and would not be stopped.

In examining the physical character of the new residential order and how it worked, it is important to understand that there were three categories of buildings that housed students.

The first consisted of the dormitories where first-year students continued to live apart. Administrative decisions determined their room assignments in Williams Hall, Sage Hall, and Lehman Hall. As before, they took their meals in Baxter Hall.

Toward the end of their first year, freshman students entered a lottery that determined their house membership for their final three years. Students were permitted to enter the lottery in groups of up to four. That feature of the new system proved to be very popular.

The second category of buildings that made up the new residential system comprised the houses with which upper class students were affiliated. These included ten former fraternity houses, all with new names, and Prospect House, along with the adjacent dining hall. Beginning in 1965, the four houses and adjacent dining areas in the Greylock Quad became part of the new system. Later, as the population of women students grew, the four houses of the Mission Park complex, with the accompanying dining areas, became part of the system in 1971.

The third component consisted of a number of large-capacity dormitories, including West College, Morgan Hall, Fayerweather, Currier, East College, and Berkshire (later renamed Fitch). Those dormitories were, in effect, annexes of the primary houses. This meant that a dormitory such as Morgan or Fayerweather offered rooms to members of numerous houses. House membership was intended to last until graduation, but the annual room draw meant that one might live in various buildings during those three years. Regardless of the location of a student's room, however, house membership defined his social life, thus determining where he dined, the intramural teams on which he played, and his participation in various house-sponsored cultural and academic events.

To achieve its mission of replacing fraternities with the new residential structure, the Standing Committee operated somewhat as a guerilla unit fighting the war one house at a time. By the spring of 1963 there had been enough progress in planning and executing the new system that the Standing Committee projected that by 1966-1967 all undergraduates would be out of fraternities and in college-operated social units.

The task of keeping score fell to Dee Gardner, though the calculations were complicated because some students who inhabited new residential houses continued as fraternity members and participated in rushing new members. Such compromises were viewed as necessary to gain the cooperation of fraternities while achieving progress in establishing the new system. Approximately a year following the release of the Angevine Committee report, Gardner responded to an inquiry from John Pritchard '57 by stating that five of the fifteen fraternities had agreed to make their houses available to the college and were cooperating in creating new residential houses, with their members typically comprising the core groups of members of the repurposed units. Three other fraternities were considering transferring their houses to the college, and the remaining seven fraternities planned to operate as usual. A few months later, on October 10, 1963, Gardner wrote Juan de Onis '48 to report that a total of eight new residential units were on line. More than half of all upperclassmen were affiliated with the new houses while also remaining members of fraternities. The fading of the old order was indisputable. Five fraternities failed to rush in the fall of 1963, and a third of the sophomore class did not participate in fraternity rushing in the fall of 1963.

A year later, in the fall of 1964, there were further indications of significant progress. Seven fraternities conducted no rush for new brothers. Of the eight that did, DKE attracted only eight new members, Zeta Psi seven, Theta Delta Chi four,

Sigma Phi two. Given their tight financial margins, there must have been wide recognition that those fraternities were doomed. Only Alpha Delta Phi (twenty-five new members), Psi U (twenty-two), and St. Anthony (sixteen) displayed vital signs that could justify any kind of optimism about the future.

Yet there remained tangled issues relating to the future of the fraternity buildings. While that task was virtually complete by 1968, the St. Anthony house, as noted earlier, was not transferred to the college until 1972. The property negotiations fell largely to a subcommittee consisting of Banks, Treasurer Charles Foehl, and Governor Jake Driscoll. Foehl in particular, with his legal training, history of dealing with the alumni fraternity corporations, and knowledge of the characteristics of the houses, was adept at negotiating transfers of those properties to the college. As a resident of Williamstown, Foehl was acutely sensitive to the fact that, as fraternity properties passed to the college, they were no longer legally liable for real estate taxes. That was true also for Mount Hope Farm, the town's largest taxpayer, after the college acquired it in 1963. Foehl's success in arranging a ten-year phase-out of municipal taxes on both the fraternity properties and Mount Hope Farm was a valuable contribution to town-and-gown relations and an important statement about the college as a responsible corporate citizen.

Some fraternities insisted that they would transfer their houses to the college only for top-dollar prices, with the idea that those proceeds would allow them to stay in business; they might purchase or build a smaller house and have money left over for operating expenses. Ted Banks recognized that to accede to that kind of arrangement would set a dangerous and expensive precedent. Meanwhile, many fraternities had adopted a watch-and-wait attitude, leasing their properties to the college and deferring long-term decisions. Some cited legal obstacles, including those imposed by the national organizations, to transferring their properties to the college. This was true of Phi Gamma Delta, the only fraternity whose house was not eventually conveyed to the college. Instead, the alumni trustees, with strong encouragement from the national fraternity officers, sold their house to the Town of Williamstown for use as a town hall.

The national Zeta Psi sued the Williams chapter in an effort to keep it from giving, selling, or leasing its house to the college. When the suit failed, Zeta Psi's alumni trustees gave the house to Williams. There was uncertainty about who would receive the money in case of a purchase, whether it should be the trustees of the local chapter, the national fraternity, or some combination. The same question arose regarding the disposition of endowment funds. The alumni trustees of the Williams chapter of Chi Psi voted to split the endowment evenly between the college and the national Chi Psi. The national Alpha Delta Phi aggressively argued that should the Williams chapter cease operations, the house and all other assets would become the property of the national. Because Alpha Delta Phi had accumulated an endowment of approximately five hundred thousand dollars, much was at stake. Allen Maulsby '44, an attorney at Cravath, Swaine, and Moore in New York volunteered his services to the college and succeeded in reaching a settlement. The AD house and 90 percent of the endowment would come to Williams.

Although there were no purchases of fraternity houses by the college, there were instances in which the college assumed outstanding mortgages, as in the case of DKE, whose new house was completed in 1962 just as fraternities were on the way out.

A number of fraternities negotiated terms that reserved certain usage rights for alumni members. Some transfer agreements forbade use of the houses as undergraduate residences. The alumni corporation of St. Anthony stubbornly demanded for several years not only that no undergraduates live in the house but also that a large residential area (the West Wing) be reserved for the exclusive use of its alumni. Theta Delta Chi president James Pilgrim '63 reported that he did not expect his fraternity's undergraduate members to oppose the Angevine Committee report, but added that some alumni factions "seem recalcitrant." A group of Theta Delta Chi alumni did indeed fiercely resist the idea of allowing its house to become a residential unit in the new system before agreeing to allow alumni and development offices to occupy their old building, while reserving certain areas for occasional use by the fraternity's alumni. Phi Delta Theta was pleased to have its house renamed in memory of its esteemed alumnus and Williams faculty member, Karl Weston. After many years as a language center, Weston House continued to be used for non-residential purposes.

Although ten former fraternity houses were integrated into the new residential system, through the years the number of the old buildings that continued to house undergraduates declined to eight. Fort Hoosac House, the former Phi Sigma Kappa fraternity house, became a dormitory to house graduate students in art history in 1982, and Bascom House, the former Beta Theta Pi house, was converted to the college's admissions headquarters in 2003.

As we survey the multiplicity of negotiations and settlements that entered into the creation of the new order, we appreciate that Ted Banks and his colleagues on the Standing Committee accomplished a task that resembled, at least in miniature form, the Peace of Westphalia in the seventeenth century. As with Westphalia, the negotiations made it possible for the warring factions to live and work together.

The 1962-1963 academic year had proven especially tumultuous, roiled by alumni anger and uncertainty over the impending changes to the fraternity system. It was particularly worrying that the ranks arrayed against the actions of the president and the trustees included some of the college's most loyal and generous alumni.

During reunion weekend in 1963, however, there were encouraging signs of growing support for the actions of the president and trustees. President Sawyer's report to the assembly of alumni in June 1963 was greeted by a prolonged standing ovation. The class of 1913, back for its fiftieth reunion, offered a strong resolution of support for the president and trustees in charting a new course for the college's residential system. The files reveal that Ted Banks, in correspondence with members of the class of 1913, had encouraged this action. Even so, the tide had clearly turned in favor of the president and trustees and the large-scale changes they were bringing to Williams.

As a trustee, Sawyer had felt that Williams was too timid in its fundraising aspirations. Now he and his trustees were boldly mapping a capital campaign whose goals dwarfed earlier efforts. President Baxter's four-million-dollar capital campaign had struggled to reach its goal in 1961, and only 34 percent of alumni contributed. Despite this new pool of funds at the end of Baxter's presidency, President Sawyer found the college's financial resources meager relative to his plans and ambitions. In his first two years he was frustrated by the failure of the larger foundations to make major commitments. Given his newness on the scene and the lack of a relevant record elsewhere, foundation officers were understandably reluctant to make substantial investments in the future of Williams. All that changed in short order, however, as President Sawyer began to unveil not only the bold commitment to transform the residential and social organization of the college, but also the purchase of Mount Hope Farm. Another exciting change was the Ten Percent admissions program, an extraordinary experiment that sought to identify applicants with unusual qualities and promise that were not reliably indicated by such criteria as grades and test scores.

At the beginning of the 1963-1964 academic year, while conflict over fraternities was still intense, President Sawyer announced a new capital campaign. Called the 175th Anniversary Fund, it established a goal of fourteen million dollars within three years and a 25.4-million-dollar total over the next ten years. Of the total, 17.5 million dollars were designated for endowment.

Governor Driscoll served as national chairman of the campaign. The formal announcement came on the weekend of October 4-5, 1963. President Sawyer asked me to give the opening speech to an assembly of some three hundred alumni, their wives, and friends of the college gathered in Jesup Hall auditorium. My purpose was to leave the alumni feeling positive about the college and confident in its future. Sawyer urged me to encourage them to ask questions so they could vent any anger and frustrations. He paced the floor at the rear of Jesup as I addressed the audience and responded to questions.

Although most questions and comments were friendly or at least not threatening, there came an accusation that Williams had a corrupting influence on its students. In responding I noted that, in view of how long students had lived at home and experienced other influences before their relatively short stay at Williams, there was hardly time for us to corrupt them. The audience laughed and appeared ready to talk about the campaign and the future of Williams.

Understandably, Sawyer had been apprehensive about how the audience would respond to an ambitious fundraising effort whose success was essential to the implementation of the Angevine Committee's recommendations. With the WAAC discouraging participation, numerous alumni declined to serve in the campaign organization, and a troubling number declared that they would not contribute. The fact that almost four hundred fewer alumni gave to the Alumni Fund in 1962-1963 than in 1961-1962 was especially worrying.

The Ford Foundation sparked the campaign with a pledge of two and a half million dollars that required matching contributions of seven and a half million dollars within three years. While the Ford commitment boosted the spirits of those who were working to carry out the Angevine Report's recommendations, it further embittered some who were fighting to preserve fraternities. An especially angry letter to President Sawyer came from William O. (Oz) Wyckoff '14, the college's recently retired director of placement and a former trustee. Wyckoff accused the president and trustees of selling out fraternities in exchange for the Ford money, ignoring that Williams was one of thirteen colleges that received Ford Foundation challenge grants at the same time.

As the fund-raising program gathered momentum, more and more alumni joined in the effort. Herbert Towne '22, troubled and confused by the Angevine Report, had reduced his usually generous Alumni Fund gift. Later he became one of the largest contributors to the capital campaign with a gift that paid for the Towne Field House. Following his death, his estate included a large bequest for Williams. And Hank Comstock '25, as Alumni Fund agent for his class, wrote to his classmates to say that while he disagreed with the trustees on the matter of fraternities, it was time for all alumni to get behind that decision and contribute financially to make Williams stronger than ever. By 1970, the 175th Anniversary Fund, with its ten-year goal of 25.4 million dollars, had raised 34 million dollars and was declared a success three years ahead of schedule.

In October 1968, the trustees resolved the issue over continuing fraternities by declaring that *all* fraternity activity must cease, effective with the graduation of the class of 1970. It had been confusing to permit what was in effect a dual citizenship arrangement whereby some students were members of both fraternities and new residential houses. By 1968 only about 10 percent of upper class students were fraternity members. While six fraternities still held meetings, none had demonstrated a credible case for allowing it to continue. There was hardly any dissent to the trustees' declaration, an action that validated the vision that Ted Banks and others held of Williams' residential and social future. When the trustees finally brought down the curtain on that one-hundred-and thirty-year chapter in the school's history, Williams was still an all-male college with an enrollment of approximately twelve hundred students. The stage was already set for a new chapter that would include the admission of women, an expansion of enrollment by about eight hundred students, a well-received new curriculum, impressive success in fund-raising, and an ambitious building program. Among its peers, Williams was poised to raise its standing significantly. Five decades later, though facing new challenges, the college is recognized nationally and internationally as a preeminent pacesetter among baccalaureate institutions.

Chapter 7
The Shape of the Present
1970 and After

Before we bid a final farewell to fraternities, it is important to acknowledge that, despite the efforts to retain most of their positive features in the new residential and social order, losses accompanied the overwhelming gains.

As skeptical as he had been about the role and value of fraternities, Mark Hopkins helped create a campus ethos of benign neglect, one that had fostered the popularity of Greek-letter secret societies. Students also used their freedom to initiate activities that were educationally valuable and contributed to their general growth. After meeting their required classroom and religious obligations, students had time to create social and literary organizations and form athletic teams and arrange intercollegiate contests. The Lyceum of Natural History, founded by a handful of students in 1835, organized scientific expeditions to such distant places as Greenland, Newfoundland, and Florida, and cooperated with famed Harvard naturalists Louis Agassiz and Asa Gray in collecting and exchanging specimens.

Hopkins regarded himself as a surrogate father to students—and many of his faculty colleagues saw him as far too indulgent with his foster children. His writings and speeches on pedagogical matters suggest, however, that he knew what he was doing. While there is plenty of evidence that some students took advantage of his disciplinary laxity, there were many who learned valuable lessons of self-reliance and social responsibility in the culture and activities beyond the bounds of the classroom.

Even after fraternities had become an impediment to the progress of Williams, there were vestiges of the positive features that older alumni gratefully remembered. The Angevine Committee itself stated in its report that it was "not unmindful" of the role of fraternities in promoting "self-discipline, social adjustment, and the assumption of responsibility." Fred Rudolph commented that the abolishment of fraternities "made for a better Williams, but bad as they were, fraternities inadvertently and accidentally in a number of ways played a role that was beneficial." He noted that, although the criteria used in selecting new members often reflected false and shallow values, the discussions of values were nevertheless important educational exercises. And communications between undergraduate and alumni fraternity brothers were effective in transmitting the college's history and traditions.

Gerry (Skip) Martin '58 was treasurer of Phi Gamma Delta just when deferred rushing was creating serious financial strains for fraternities. Reported Martin, "I learned a lot about how a small business is run. I was responsible for collections, budgeting and meeting a payroll. If I failed in any of these responsibilities I had to answer to the rest of the house and the parents who paid their sons' house bills." Martin noted that while occasionally fraternity officers might seek counsel from deans or parents, for the most part they were on their own in resolving the problems for which they were responsible. Carl Vogt '58, president of Phi Gamma Delta while Martin was treasurer, agreed with Martin that, while it was past time for fraternities to go, they retained certain virtues even at the end of their long history. He pointed to the concern fraternity brothers had for one another, expressed not only in the disciplinary authority that he and other fraternity officers sometimes exerted when a member was disruptive to the common life of the brotherhood, but also in the counseling and advice they offered to troubled brethren.

Today Williams is far past the point when nostalgia for fraternities makes any sense. But it is always relevant for liberal arts colleges to ask how best to promote student self-reliance and a sense of responsibility for the collective good that fraternities, in their best moments, encouraged and that have always been recognized as marks of a liberally educated person.

140

As one would expect, constantly changing circumstances meant that even after the final abolition of fraternities in 1970 the new residential, dining, and social system remained a work in progress. In anticipation of the arrival of women students, the Mission Park complex, completed in 1971, increased living quarters by 314 beds and included new dining facilities. During the transition from the Sawyer to the Chandler administrations in 1973-1974, the college repossessed the old Williams Inn; renamed Dodd House, it would house fifty-seven students and provide another dining hall. A number of conversions and additions involving various small buildings provided approximately one hundred more beds. By 2012, Williams-owned facilities provided space for 1,970 undergraduates, while up to 150 seniors were permitted to live off-campus.

The new cafeteria-style dining spaces in the Greylock complex, Driscoll Hall, and Mission Park led to the gradual elimination of the old fraternity dining halls, with the final four closing in 1980. The popularity of the new dining facilities of Paresky Center (2007), combined with financial retrenchment, led in turn to the decision to close the Greylock dining areas, along with limiting the use of the Dodd House dining hall to special occasions.

Various forces were at work in producing a surplus of dining space. One was the availability of a variety of dining plans that allowed students to have as few as seven meals a week in college dining halls rather than the standard twenty-one of earlier eras. Perhaps an even more important factor was a shift in the dining culture. The long, lingering meals that fraternity members enjoyed and that carried forward into the early post-fraternity era gradually evolved into a grab-gobble-go pattern that ensured a turnover rate comparable to that of a fast-food restaurant.

After the early shakedown phase, the new structure that the Standing Committee had created operated successfully for about three decades. It became apparent during the 1990s, however, that adaptations had gradually reshaped the system in ways that had led to radical departures from its original design and purposes. The disintegration began with attempts to be more accommodating to students who seemed to have good reasons for wanting to change house membership. That quickly devolved into a practice of free agency that effectively put all rooms up for grabs every year. Free agency facilitated the ease with which the room assignment process could be manipulated so as to create large blocs of students with similar interests, such as athletic teams. Clearly, such results were at odds with the Standing Committee's vision of a campus where students from a variety of backgrounds and with disparate interests would live with and learn from their peers. The aim had been to make all residential houses generally representative of the overall campus population, as well as places where small groups of close friends could live together, enjoy the same parties, play on the same intramural teams, and experience the common life of their houses.

Following a few years of uncontested free agency, the Committee on Undergraduate Life (CUL) struggled for nearly a decade, beginning in the mid-1990s, with a succession of efforts to restore the essential substance and spirit of the original house system. Professors Charles Dew and Will Dudley led those initiatives as successive chairs of the CUL. The CUL devised first the cluster house system, then the anchor system, followed by the neighborhood system. Strong and steady student resistance led in each case to relatively minor revisions and name changes that amounted to little more than a succession of synonyms for what in actual practice was a slightly modified system of free agency. The core concept throughout the reform efforts was that students, through a lottery draw, would be assigned permanently to a housing complex. While they might move to a different unit in the same complex they would not be permitted to move to a house in a different complex. At least that was the intention.

As the system design stood in 2012, students, beginning with the sophomore year, were assigned to one of twenty-five houses based upon a room-draw in which individuals and groups of up to six listed their preferences. The houses were divided up among four neighborhoods (Dodd, Spencer, Wood, and Currier). Thus the neighborhood in which a student lived was the consequence of the house choice, not the other way around. The number of beds in those neighborhoods ranged from 257 to 347. Seniors who lived in non-college housing and students who lived in coop houses where residents prepared their own meals were also members of a neighborhood.

Each of the neighborhoods had a budget that supported various group activities, including—importantly—social events. The elected student officers of the neighborhoods included a treasurer and a programming coordinator. Each neighborhood also had a program director, a faculty member who acted as a general advisor to the neighborhood officers and suggested programs that often involved faculty participation. Thus mathematics professor Frank Morgan was the Dodd neighborhood faculty program director and a member of the Dodd governance board. As such, his was the principal voice in proposing programs that involved faculty and staff members.

Professor Morgan's main project for academic year 2012-2013 was a series of monthly student-faculty dinners. Faculty participants were invited in departmental groups. In addition to the dinnertime conversations among groups of faculty and students, the evening's program often included a brief talk and discussion led by one or more faculty members. While Dodd neighborhood dinners bore a certain resemblance to fraternity dinners of long ago, they illustrated more convincingly than fraternity social events, and even the social activities sponsored by residential houses in the early post-fraternity years, how to integrate student residential and social life with the college's academic mission.

On paper, the neighborhood system as it was officially presented in 2012 had a pleasing logic and symmetry as a way of organizing student living, dining, and social arrangements. Still, the overwhelming testimony of students and faculty indicated that it was not unusual for students to live in as many as three different neighborhoods during their upper class years because of the jockeying for the best possible room. Thus, there was a perpetual musical chairs movement that differed little from the free agency that the neighborhoods were supposed to replace. Those conditions did not foster the kind of identification with and sense of loyalty to one's house and neighborhood that had been intended.

Reflecting back on his experience as chair of the Committee on Undergraduate Life, Charles Dew stated that it was naïve of him and his committee colleagues to think that over time students would buy into the neighborhood concept. Still, he concluded, the work of the CUL had been valuable in identifying and correcting extreme cases in which the membership of certain houses consisted exclusively or almost entirely of self-selected groups defined by particular interests or specific racial, ethnic, or gender identities. There were, for example, instances in which many members of the same athletic team lived together. There were also instances in which students who lived together tended to stick together in their choices of courses. To permit students to go through college encased in comfortable residential and curricular cocoons was clearly at odds with the purposes of residential liberal education.

But did it matter that the efforts of the past twenty years to restore the character and effectiveness of the residential organization that the Standing Committee created did not succeed?

The Angevine Committee and the Standing Committee had understandably emphasized the role of residential arrangements in facilitating the processes by which students learn from one another, and, even as they were abolishing fraternities, the fraternity model of residential life was foremost in their minds. Though social arrangements would necessarily remain a component of the overall educational experience at Williams, the college has long since moved in the direction of subordinating residential considerations to pedagogical and curricular factors. Indeed, that shift had been implicit in the campaign against fraternities, with the recognition that fraternity culture had long overborne the college's educational mission. With abolition, the center of college life shifted from the fraternity house or dormitory to the lecture hall, the seminar room, the laboratory, library, and beyond, making questions of residential organization of lesser import.

The transformation had been swift and dramatic. Within a decade or two, Williams, so long known as a country club school dominated by decadent fraternities, became one of the leading liberal arts colleges in the United States, highly regarded for its rigorous academic standards and tough admissions requirements. The number of applicants for a place at the college increased as the school became one of the most selective in the nation, welcoming a population of students far more diverse than Tyler Dennett could ever have imagined—or perhaps would have desired.

The new Williams was unmistakably modern, thanks in no small part to Jack Sawyer's vision of what the college might become when liberated from the anti-intellectual weight of fraternities. Sawyer's Plans and Purposes became the founding document of the new Williams. Apart from the specific proposals, which would come to define the college's curriculum and its academic temper, raising both faculty standards and student expectations, Sawyer's vision encouraged boldness and innovation in education, a Jeffersonian recognition that the life of the mind must keep up with its times, that periodic revolutions in thought were both inevitable and salutary, that the ultimate aim of education was the creation of leaders suited to their time and place, be they the republican yeomen of Western Massachusetts who attended Williams in the early nineteenth century or the global citizens of the early twenty-first century.

To grasp the potential of global citizenship at Williams today, one must take into account the remarkable diversity of the contemporary campus. Compare, for instance, the current socioeconomic profile of the undergraduate population compared with that of the Sawyer era, as measured by financial aid. In 2012, about 53 percent of students received financial aid, as compared with approximately 25 percent in Sawyer's time. That pointed to significant outreach to the financially challenged, a greater effort by the college to find and enroll Dennett's cross-section of Americans. Even so, Williams and most of its peers still fell short in attracting high-ability students from the bottom 40 percent of the economic strata. Research studies, including widely cited publications by Williams economists, pointed to the likelihood that the future of Williams would include still more students from that segment of the U.S. population.

The varied new face of the college extended to religion, which for so long had been at the core of the Williams identity. In 1883, President Franklin Carter appointed the first college chaplain, John H. Denison, a Congregational minister from the class of 1862. Up through the era of Mark Hopkins, himself a minister, so many members of the faculty were ordained Congregational ministers that there hardly seemed to be any point in having a chaplain.

In 2012, the supervisory chaplain was a Protestant minister, in keeping with a long tradition and consistent with the religious composition of the student body until well after Sawyer's era. But now the college employs other chaplains as well, including a Roman Catholic, a Jew, and a Muslim. During the administration of President Francis Oakley (1985-1993), the college built the Jewish Religious Center to serve the sizeable population of Jewish students, faculty, and staff.

The Williams curriculum had earlier reflected the backgrounds, interests, history, and probable futures of the white, male, and largely Protestant make-up of the student body. But with the broad socioeconomic, racial, religious, gender, and nationality diversity of the current students and faculty, including between 7 and 8 percent of foreign nationals in the student body, compared with a tiny handful in 1960s, the curriculum of the early twenty-first century evolved to accommodate wider interests and aspirations, reflected in the rising number of courses and programs in identity studies and in the appointment of faculty specialists in such fields.

This great increase in the diversity of the Williams community would, in a seeming paradox, generate strong cultural and psychological forces that propelled students toward tighter bonding with those who shared their backgrounds, interests, and lifestyles. They would instinctively attempt to recreate, in some form, the exclusivity of the old fraternity culture. In such an environment, the challenge of motivating students to learn about

146

and from peers unlike them, that is, to educate them for global citizenship, became steeper. The demonstrated difficulty of achieving that goal by simply reforming residential arrangements underscored the importance of placing greater emphasis on styles and strategies of academic learning as a means of achieving a closer and more cohesive student community. Fortunately, late twentieth-century Williams had evolved a strong foundation of traditions and experience both conventional and unconventional for moving more aggressively in that direction.

The late Robert Gaudino (1925-1974), professor of political science, stressed that life's most important lessons came from "uncomfortable learning." The growing emphasis at Williams on experiential education underscored the need to offer more educational experiences that took students outside their comfort zones and into learning experiences that combined scholarly inquiry, analysis, and reflection with social and civic engagement. That is what Gaudino sought in courses that took students to remote villages in India and into homes in Southern Appalachia, the American South, working class neighborhoods in Detroit, and farm families in Iowa.

The Winter Study program, inaugurated in 1968, has made many valuable contributions of the sort that Gaudino advocated and exemplified. The long-established course Eye Care and Culture on the Atlantic Coast of Nicaragua illustrated the potential for such offerings. Originated by retired athletic director Robert Peck in 2002, and with the collaboration of the New England College of Optometry, the course trained Williams students to prescribe and dispense eye glasses to the inhabitants of remote and impoverished villages in Nicaragua. That activity, under demanding and physically strenuous conditions, required students to be closely interdependent and provided them access to population groups whose needs they helped to meet and whose cultures they were able to observe and study. Today there is far greater student demand for entry to such courses than the spots available. Increases in the budget for Winter Study would make it possible to offer many more courses that involve travel and that are similar in method and aims to Eye Care and Culture.

147

The World Travel Fellowships program, underwritten by the class of 1945 and with an endowment fund now valued at twelve million dollars, made special use of the summer months and illustrated anew the learning potential of encountering unfamiliar cultures under challenging circumstances. Although Williams does not offer summer courses to its undergraduates for credit, the natural sciences and mathematics departments in particular have also made imaginative use of the summer months to enrich the overall educational experience of students. Relevant committees at Williams are considering whether some of the summertime projects might be awarded the same academic credit as Winter Study courses. The summer programs place great emphasis on working as teams, an approach to academic work that is increasingly popular. They bring together students who might not otherwise have become acquainted and enable them to work together.

The rich tapestry of social interactions and intellectual engagement among students in the varied settings of field trips, social service activities, classrooms, laboratories, libraries, theatres, dance studios, and athletic facilities presents a picture of incessant encounters with other students, as well as faculty and staff members. Many of those encounters will remain superficial, but some are likely to be long-lasting, profound, and life-altering. The numerous wedding pictures in alumni publications demonstrate the astonishing frequency with which campus friendships flower into life partnerships. The homing instinct that motivates alumni to provide generous financial support to Williams and which brings them back to the campus for reunions attests powerfully to the influence of their Williams experience. Fifty years ago, returning alumni headed immediately to their fraternity houses. Now they rejoice in the company of a far broader range of classmates and friends.

Let us turn back now to those developments initiated a half-century ago that led to the transformation of Williams, fulfilling the dreams and hopes of the pioneers who took the first steps. Imagine that John Sawyer had conformed to the perceptions of those who saw him as too cautious and conservative to take bold and visionary steps and that he had settled for minor adjustments to the fraternity system rather than its total replacement. Or we might, with greater plausibility, imagine him launching a series of incremental steps with the ultimate goal of phasing out fraternities.

As President Sawyer spelled out his vision for a renewed Williams, alumni sentiment increasingly supported the Angevine Committee's recommendations.

Had he and his trustees chosen either of these alternatives, the strong likelihood is that there would have been a messy, prolonged period of disintegration of residential life, as Professor Gates had feared. Some fraternities would probably have retained open membership and evolved into clubs. It is likely that the stronger houses would have gone in the opposite direction, becoming even more pronounced in their adherence to traditional norms and processes of fraternity membership selection. The campus and the alumni body would have become more polarized, and the ethos of inclusiveness would have been compromised by the ever-present centrifugal impulses that tend towards caste-based neighborhoods instead of cohesive communities of diverse individuals.

The admission and assimilation of women would almost certainly have been a far less orderly and successful process. College officers, trustees, faculty members, and students would have spent more time than ever dealing with problems related to residential and social life and thus less time planning, promoting,

149

and experiencing a vigorous, exciting learning culture for global citizenship.

Such scenarios did not unfold because Sawyer's vision, intelligence, and courage were equal to the occasion. If he had conflicting thoughts and emotions regarding whether to proceed as he did or to take a more measured pace, the subsequent history of Williams has made clear that he obeyed the right instincts. Despite all the suffering that he bore from the forced-march approach to the transforming changes, it was fortunate that he and the trustees chose to proceed in that fashion rather than in a slower and more deliberate way.

When I spoke at his memorial service in January 1995, my remarks included the statement that John Sawyer was, along with Mark Hopkins, the most transforming president in Williams' history. I know more about Mark Hopkins now than I did then. I regard him as a great teacher with remarkable pedagogical insights, as President James A. Garfield so graphically summarized in his immortal aphorism, "The ideal college is Mark Hopkins on one end of a log and a student on the other." Still, as his faculty colleague John Bascom and other critics noted, he also allowed Williams to fall behind its peers in important ways.

With no qualifications of any kind, my conclusion now is that Sawyer was the most transforming leader in Williams' history. Hardly any dimension of the college's operation was left unaltered by his tenure. He initiated many imaginative changes, large and small. He vastly expanded the college's financial resources. The carefully planned and skillfully executed operation that resulted in bringing women to Williams and almost doubling its size was perhaps the smoothest such transition among the many that occurred during that period. His energy and initiative resulted in a curriculum structure that included the innovative Winter Study program and added numerous new academic programs and fields of study, all of which helped make Williams a leader in liberal arts education.

AFTERWORD
The Williams Model and the Lingering Legacy of the Greeks

During the half-century since the Angevine Report appeared, members of the Williams community have continually expressed surprise that the Williams example failed to attract a larger and more immediate following among other liberal arts colleges with a strong fraternity presence. That surprise has been accompanied by pride in the unwavering leadership demonstrated by President Sawyer and the trustees. Yet a comprehensive review would show that, in fact, the role of fraternities and sororities at liberal arts colleges has steadily declined over the past fifty years. The brief review that follows focuses upon developments at a small number of similar institutions that are geographically proximate to Williams College.

The first institution to study closely the Williams example and adopt a policy modeled on it was Colby College. Colby president William Cotter (1979-2000) gained a thorough knowledge of the Williams experience through conversations and campus visits. In 1984, the Colby trustees prohibited further undergraduate fraternity and sorority activity both on and off campus. As the 2012 Colby Student Handbook explained, fraternities and sororities were inconsistent with "many of the fundamental values to which the community subscribes."

At the invitation of President Robert Edwards (1990-2001) and the Bowdoin trustees, I assisted with a study of the Bowdoin's fraternity-dominated residential system, as well as its bicameral governing board. The issues relating to residential life were far more complicated and took longer to resolve than those having to do with the governance structure. The eventual outcome was the decision, in March 1997, to replace the fraternities with a house system. Under the heading Fraternity Membership Policy, the 2013 Bowdoin Student Handbook stated,

151

"Students involved in rushing, pledging, perpetrating, and initiating activities by fraternities and similar selective-membership social organizations will be dismissed permanently from Bowdoin College." Bowdoin phased out existing fraternities over a period of three years; though there was to be no pledging of new members, old members might remain active until their classes graduated. During the same period Bowdoin acquired all fraternity houses and integrated them into the residential system.

The trustees of Middlebury College voted in 1990 to abolish single-sex social organizations. Sororities had ceased to exist some thirty years earlier, but fraternities continued to flourish. Told they might continue only if they agreed to admit women, some so agreed, but others chose to disband. Delta Kappa Epsilon decided to fight the college in a Vermont court on the ground that the trustees' decision denied its members their First Amendment right of free association. DKE lost its case when the Addison County Superior Court ruled that Middlebury College was a private institution instead of a "state actor" and thus had made "a valid and permissible decision to create an academic environment that would eliminate gender based distinctions that have historically limited a woman's opportunity to develop her individual talents and participate more fully in a free and open society." In denying the claims of DKE, the court also rejected the claim that Middlebury's policy interfered with the plaintiff's freedom of speech. Fraternities remained free to debate issues, "including the wisdom of the current college policy." The court verdict prompted some fraternities to go underground, but the college's policy remained in place and was generally effective.

Hamilton College faced serious litigation when it chose to close fraternity houses. A federal lawsuit initiated in 1995 by four fraternities claimed that by denying their members the right to live and dine in fraternity houses, and by requiring them to live and dine instead in college-owned facilities, the college was acting in restraint of trade and therefore violating the Sherman Antitrust Act.

The Hamilton legal saga began with the decision to require sophomore fraternity members to live in college-owned residences for at least the academic year 1993-1994. The Hamilton trustees later decreed that, effective in September 1995, all students must live in college-owned housing and participate in a college meal plan. Hamilton then set out to purchase the fraternity houses. The fraternity plaintiffs argued that the college's actions created monopolistic control over student housing in the small town of Clinton, New York (population 2,000). Moreover, because Hamilton College was the only market for the purchase of the fraternity houses, the fraternities were forced to sell at the college's price.

The U.S. District Court for the Northern District of New York promptly dismissed the claims. The Court of Appeals for the Second Circuit, however, reversed the district court decision, noting that such activities as bookstore operations, athletic programs, tuition setting, and financial aid awards were definitely commercial and thus subject to the requirements of the Sherman Act.

Despite this development, three of the four plaintiff fraternities were forced to settle with the college because of unaffordable legal expenses. Sigma Phi, the richest of the four, chose to take the case back to district court. The magistrate judge assigned to the case issued a summary judgment in favor of Hamilton College on the ground that the college lacked "market power" in the relevant market.

Despite the legal victory, Hamilton itself was left bitterly divided, the plaintiff fraternities financially weakened, and the final ruling questioned by some legal scholars. Overall, however, as at Williams, the college gained in quality and reputation following the curtailment of fraternity and sorority life, and competition for admission grew much more intense.

During its 2011-2012 bicentennial celebration, Hamilton gave a proud account of its first two centuries. The college by then had gained ownership of all the former fraternity properties, whose physical appearance it vastly improved. The Greek names had been replaced by the names of notable persons in Hamilton's history. Fraternities and sororities continued to exist, and though they did not have their own living and dining quarters, they had

153

the reputation of giving the best parties on campus, which by college policy were open to all students. In 2012, inquiries to Hamilton students suggested that Greek organizations had come to resemble other campus clubs in some respects.

Still, catch-as-catch-can conversations with a limited number of Hamilton students indicated that serious Greek life issues remained. Fraternities and sororities were exclusive organizations that chose their own members, and many students questioned the criteria and values that guided those choices. Hazing and alcohol abuse were cited as problems. While first-year students were blended with upper class students in college dormitories, a newly approved plan provided for clusters of first-year students to inhabit particular floors or other dormitory areas. Presumably, the new plan had the goal of fostering a stronger sense of class identity. Whether the intention was also to weaken the appeal of Greek membership was not clear. Perhaps the evolution of Greek life at Hamilton over the past fifteen years conformed generally to what Jay Angevine had in mind with his description of "continuing fraternities." The Hamilton model also illustrated the problems Ted Banks perceived in that concept and that led to the Williams goal of total elimination of fraternities.

Against the expectations of administrators, fraternities also continued at Wesleyan University, in Middletown, Connecticut, and even though they gradually devolved into a minor element of campus life, they remained a source of concern for the university. At Wesleyan, there was the added complication of sororities. Wesleyan was founded in 1831 as an all-male college, and fraternities came to play a lively role on campus. But the school started admitting women in 1872, and with them came sororities. In 1909, when Wesleyan's board became uncomfortable with the "experiment" that brought women to the campus, the university returned to its all-male, fraternity-dominated culture, only to reverse course once more in 1970, when it again began to accept women.

Fraternities and sororities had flourished together at Wesleyan during the late nineteenth and early twentieth centuries. But in the 1960s and after, both went into a decline so steep that Wesleyan's trustees and successive presidents saw no need to take the kind of radical steps that Williams instituted after the Angevine Report. Although many believed that fraternities at Wesleyan would die out, that did not happen.

Depending on how they were defined, as few as six or as many as a dozen endured at Wesleyan. Some who cited the larger numbers included on the lists four ethnic sororities and the Latino Brotherhood. Other sources limited their list to about six fraternities and one sorority. But if one counted only secretive societies as fraternities or sororities, the number would appear to be about four. Organizations whose membership criteria variously included ethnic, racial, and gender identity would be regarded on many campuses as clubs, not fraternities or sororities.

Another aspect of the Wesleyan scene was that it included fraternities that existed for a century or more but which had abandoned their rituals and made no pretense of being secret societies. Regardless of the criteria used, there seemed to be general agreement that membership in what were regarded as fraternities and sororities comprised relatively few students, numbering below 10 percent of Wesleyan undergraduates. Still, the parties of some organizations generated considerable attention because of the crowds they drew, including many non-members. On some occasions, rowdy parties brought complaints from townspeople and resulted in interventions from the campus security force and town police officers.

In early February 2011, Wesleyan announced that, beginning in August 2011, its students would be prohibited from participating in social activities on properties owned, leased, or operated "by private societies that are not recognized by the University." That decision provoked an outpouring of responses from students, parents of students, and alumni, with the common theme that it was none of the university's business where or how students lived, along with many references to First Amendment rights. President Michael Roth followed up with a new message on February 24 that made clear that the University's particular concern was the status of Beta Theta Pi fraternity, an unregistered fraternity.

Established at Wesleyan in 1890, Beta seemed to be a Wesleyan organization, yet the university had no oversight of its house. By establishing the new policy, Wesleyan sought to remove what it termed a "dangerous ambiguity" by encouraging Beta "to join the other fraternities and sororities in working together with the school" and by preventing "similar situations from arising in the future with private homes adjacent to campus."

The reason for the university's urgency was unmentioned in Roth's statement. A few months before, a first-year student alleged that she had been raped at a Halloween party at the Beta Theta Pi house by a man who was not a student but was a friend of a Beta member, and that Wesleyan students at the party had taunted her. In October 2012, the anonymous woman sued Wesleyan and its chapter of Beta Theta Pi in federal district court, alleging that the university had been well aware of Beta house's reputation as a "rape factory" and had failed to take effective actions to control it. The civil case, in which the plaintiff had sought ten million dollars in damages, was settled in August 2013 on undisclosed terms. The earlier trial of the alleged rapist had resulted in an uncontested verdict of guilty on a reduced charge and a prison sentence of fifteen months.

Beta Theta Pi, whose house was off-campus, had refused to comply with the university's requirements that fraternities with houses register with the university and allow inspections to insure that adequate living conditions were provided. The policy announced in February 2011 recognized, perhaps belatedly, that university officers and trustees would be neglecting their fiduciary responsibilities were they not to take necessary measures to protect the health and safety of students, thereby leaving the university legally and morally vulnerable.

Schools without Greek societies, such as Williams, were not immune from incidents such as that involving the Beta fraternity at Wesleyan, but the presence of a fraternity culture seemed clearly to elevate the risks. The Wesleyan experience with Beta Theta Pi underscored again the wisdom of the Williams trustees in establishing residential regulations on a foundation of educational goals.

Inevitably, Williams people over the years have considered the contrasts between Williams and Amherst in dealing with fraternity issues.

In the spring of 1959, an enterprising *Williams Record* reporter, Ted Castle '60, ventured to Amherst to look at the fraternity scene. An article published on April 15, 1959 stressed the central point that, by Williams standards, only about three Amherst fraternities qualified as true fraternities. Pledging of black students and Jews was routine, with little fuss or notice. The difference in dining arrangements was a crucial factor. Since 1941, all Amherst students had dined in a central facility, Valentine Hall. Castle noted that although Amherst permitted fraternities to reserve tables for their members, "Few fraternities have arranged a time and place in the dining hall for meals. In the cases where there is a house table, only some of the members eat with the house anyway. This is probably the greatest cause for the non-fraternity spirit at Amherst." This lack of commitment to Greek life was manifested in the high dropout rate among Amherst fraternity members, in contrast with a low number of resignations from Williams fraternities.

Especially interesting was Castle's observation that "Amherst is becoming through admissions policy, curriculum direction and social organization a school of heterogeneous students whose common basis of association is a high level of intelligence." That comment lent credence to the conclusion of the Angevine Committee three years later that the overall environment in many of the Williams fraternities made it difficult for students to do serious academic work in their living quarters.

Three years after Castle's article, and almost simultaneous to the release of the Angevine Committee report, Amherst president Calvin Plimpton announced, with negligible attention or questioning, that the college was assuming responsibility for fraternity real estate taxes and property insurance. In return, the college took title to the fraternity houses and then turned around and leased them back to the alumni fraternity corporations. It was a clever move that seemed to make everyone a winner. In addition, Amherst trustees approved the construction of a group of "social dorms" that were to have many of the amenities and attractions of fraternity houses. By these actions Amherst did not ban fraternities, but it further lowered their profile. As Ted Castle's observations indicated, fraternities at Amherst simply did not present the problems that perpetually agitated the Williams campus.

Approximately two decades later, in February 1984, the advantage of the leverage that the Amherst president and trustees had gained was dramatically illustrated when Acting President G. Armour Craig announced the abolition of fraternities, effective four months later, at the close of the academic year. A universally loved and admired English professor, Craig was the choice of the trustees to lead Amherst when President Julian Gibbs died of a heart attack while skiing on February 20, 1983. During Craig's transitional presidency, he and the board agreed that the time had come to abolish fraternities. Because of his standing with all the college's constituencies, Craig was the ideal choice to spearhead that effort. An ad hoc trustee committee headed by Charles Longsworth, former president of Hampshire College, did some polling of alumni that indicated there was enough support for abolishing fraternities to justify the risk. Still, it was realistic to expect some opposition from both students and alumni.

When Amherst considered the Williams example, it found that its rival was rapidly catching up on the money front and its academic reputation was soaring. Moreover, the transition to coeducation had gone very smoothly, more so than at Amherst, which started a half-decade later and with fraternities as a complicating factor. All the Amherst fraternities eventually admitted women students as members, but Longsworth reported that they were often ill at ease and treated like second-class citizens. Fraternities welcomed them largely because of undersubscribed membership rosters and empty rooms.

Amherst and Williams had been watching one another like hawks since 1821. From the Amherst perspective in 1984, Williams appeared to be in very good shape academically, financially, and socially, and the elimination of fraternities seemed to have much to do with that picture. As Amherst

158

followed the Williams example, Armour Craig carried the message, bringing with him attendant good will. While the fraternity announcement was greeted warmly by faculty and many others, it proved upsetting to fraternity stalwarts. Yet it also left unbesmirched the new president, Peter Pouncey, formerly dean of Columbia College of Columbia University. With the deed done by Craig, Pouncey was free to lead the college into a new era. Pouncey took office as the permanent successor to President Gibbs on July 1, 1984, one day after the ban on fraternities took effect. In the ongoing chess match that always marked relations between Williams and Amherst, Amherst had made a succession of bold and brilliant catch-up moves.

President Jack Sawyer had been well aware of Amherst's approach to fraternity issues during the presidency of Calvin Plimpton (1960-1971), and he heard from many Williams alumni who noted with approval the Amherst model. In a letter to alumnus John Redfield '19 Sawyer conceded that Amherst had acted more adroitly than Williams in the way it acquired control over fraternity properties. Sawyer also noted, however, that Amherst had more money than Williams and thus could afford options not open to Williams. For instance, the Sterling Committee had considered the possibility of building a central dining hall, and it is likely that President Baxter and the trustees viewed such a move as financially unaffordable. They might also have argued convincingly that denial of dining revenues would be financially ruinous to the fraternities. Like it or not, Williams and the fraternities were symbiotically linked, and the surgery to separate them would be drastic, regardless of whether it occurred as a single procedure or over an extended period. Ted Castle was right about the differences between the two colleges with respect to fraternities. The Williams approach was appropriate to its unique circumstances. And the end result was remarkably successful.

The Amherst decision to end the fraternity era wasn't an overnight success. Predictably, some Amherst fraternities went underground in the wake of the sudden decision to ban them in 1984. The thrust of the new Amherst policy was prohibition of on-campus fraternity activity, and that policy was seriously enforced from the beginning. The relevant language in the 2012 Student Handbook was straightforward, stern, and sweeping. It declared that "no resource of the college (physical, staff, or monetary) shall be used or employed, directly or indirectly, in any procedure relating to rushing, pledging, initiating or otherwise admitting to or maintaining membership by any student of the college in any fraternity, sorority or other social club, society or organization (however denominated)."

Off-campus fraternity activity was another matter. While growling noises from Amherst authorities seemed to have a suppressing effect, there was no pretense that off-campus fraternity activity could be completely stopped. In a region more populous than the Berkshires, there were numerous hiding places, including next door at the University of Massachusetts-Amherst, with its fraternity culture. Amherst College students were generally disapproving of attempts to subvert the spirit of the college policy, and those who defied the fraternity ban were usually careful to keep that information to themselves.

Still, there were occasional reminders of the ambiguities and liabilities of a policy that banned on-campus fraternities but turned a blind eye to surreptitious fraternity activity off-campus. In the autumn of 2012, Amherst College received unwanted national publicity and faced on-campus turmoil when there were serious accusations of sexual assaults by male students against women students, accompanied by the claim that relevant administrators were lax in responding to those charges. A widely circulated cartoon that originated with an off-campus underground fraternity presented an offensive and demeaning view of female students as sexual objects. The episode illustrated the difficulty of cleanly separating on-campus and off-campus student behavior when the behavior in question is at odds with the spirit and substance of college rules and policies.

It is interesting to note how common it was for underground fraternity activity to occur when fraternities were banned. That occurred at Williams when, late in Sawyer's administration and for several years in my administration, two secret fraternities, led by alumni members, operated in houses in Pownal, Vermont. Unlike the Amherst experience, the outlaw fraternities did not survive. Stern warnings to students who were involved, a general lack of undergraduate interest, and minimal alumni support resulted in abandonment of these efforts to keep fraternities alive. One of the houses burned down, and the other was sold at auction for failure to pay real estate taxes.

The Greylock Quad would be part of the new Williams. The goal was, according to the Angevine Committee, "a campus where education, in its broadest sense, would take place everywhere and at all times."

Another common development was litigation, as illustrated by suits against Middlebury and Hamilton. In several instances, a few years after the banning of fraternities, Williams was threatened with lawsuits on grounds of First Amendment violations. Campus turmoil during the 1960s, much of it related to the Civil Rights and Vietnam War struggles, sometimes resulted in interventions by courts and law enforcement authorities at the behest of college and university authorities. That, in turn, led to a general decline in the long-established reticence by judges and police to become involved with the internal affairs of universities. College presidents and trustees understandably became more cautious about embarking on the kind of bold initiatives that Williams undertook following the recommendations of the Angevine Committee. Williams was fortunate in the timing of its action, but it was also fortunate in that none of the threatened lawsuits materialized. The most

161

critical factors, however, were the vision, courage, and resolve of President John Sawyer and the trustees.

After a decade of remarkable leadership and achievement, everyone concerned with Williams would have understood had Sawyer decided to rest on his oars and let the considerable momentum he had generated carry him into a well-deserved retirement. Instead, he continued for two more productive years as he planned and raised money for a new library, built the Mission Park dormitory complex, and founded the New England Small College Athletic Conference (NESCAC).

The transformation of Williams College under Sawyer's leadership was breathtakingly comprehensive in its scope. The elimination of fraternities, however, was the key to his accomplishments and his crowning achievement.

APPENDICES

WILLIAMS FRATERNITIES BY YEAR OF ESTABLISHMENT

PRESIDENT EDWARD DORR GRIFFIN (1821-1836)
Kappa Alpha (1833)
Sigma Phi (1834)
Delta Upsilon (1834; dissolved in 1864; revived in 1883)

PRESIDENT MARK HOPKINS (1836-1872)
Chi Psi (1842)
Beta Theta Pi (1847; dissolved in 1851; revived in 1914 when Psi
Omega, established in 1912, is awarded the Beta Theta Pi charter)

Zeta Psi (1847; goes inactive in 1848; revived in 1881))
Alpha Delta Phi (1851)
Delta Psi/St. Anthony (1853)
Delta Kappa Epsilon (1855)

PRESIDENT PAUL ANSEL CHADBOURNE (1872-1881)
Phi Gamma Delta (1880; became dormant almost immediately;
revived in 1913 when a local fraternity, Alpha Zeta Alpha,
founded in 1903, was awarded the Phi Gamma Delta charter)

PRESIDENT FRANKLIN CARTER (1881-1901)
Phi Delta Theta (1886)
Theta Delta Chi (1891)

PRESIDENT HENRY HOPKINS (1902-1908)
Phi Sigma Kappa (1906)

PRESIDENT HARRY GARFIELD (1908-1934)
Psi Upsilon (1913)
Delta Phi (1926)

NEW WILLIAMS FRATERNITY HOUSES: 1881-1961

(Includes only houses of fraternities extant in 1962)

PRESIDENT FRANKLIN CARTER (1881-1901)
Delta Psi (Saint Anthony) (CDE) (1886)
Alpha Delta Phi (Perry) (1895)
Sigma Phi (Van Rensselaer) (1895; dismantled in 1973 for
construction of Sawyer Library)
Delta Kappa Epsilon (1898; destroyed by fire in January 1959,
replaced by new DKE house in 1961

PRESIDENT HENRY HOPKINS (1902-1908)
Phi Delta Theta (Weston) (1907)
Zeta Psi (Wood) (1907)
Kappa Alpha (purchased from William Alexander Procter estate
in 1907; destroyed by fire in January 1968)

PRESIDENT HARRY GARFIELD (1908-1934)
Chi Psi (Spencer) (1909)
Beta Theta Pi (Bascom) (1913)
Delta Upsilon (James A. Garfield House) (purchased in 1924)
Theta Delta Chi (Mears) (1926)
Psi Upsilon (Tyler) (1927)
Phi Gamma Delta (Town Hall) (1928)
Phi Sigma Kappa (Taconic) (1931)

PRESIDENT JAMES PHINNEY BAXTER (1937-1961)
Delta Kappa Epsilon (Brooks) (1961)
Delta Phi (Agard) (1906, purchased by fraternity in 1951)
Phi Sigma Kappa (Ft. Hoosac/Taconic) (1931)

NEW WILLIAMS BUILDINGS: 1881-1934

PRESIDENT FRANKLIN CARTER (1881-1901)
(old) Clark Hall (1881)
Morgan Hall (1882)
Lasell Gymnasium (1886)
Thompson Biology (1893)
Thompson Chemistry (1893)
Thompson Physics (1893)
Hopkins Hall (1890)
Jesup Hall (1899)

PRESIDENT HENRY HOPKINS (1902-1908)
Berkshire Hall (now Fitch House) (1905)
Thompson Memorial Chapel (1905)
(new) Clark Hall (Geology) (1908)

PRESIDENT HARRY GARFIELD (1908-1934)
Currier Hall (1908)
Thompson Hall (infirmary) (1911)
Williams Hall (1911)
Chapin Hall (1912)
Stetson Hall (1922)
Sage Hall (1923)
Cole Field House (1926)
Lehman Hall (1928)
Heating Plant (1934)

Notes: The trustees approved the construction of Clark Hall in January 1908 at the end of Henry Hopkins' administration. The building was dedicated at the beginning of the Garfield administration in October 1908. The trustees approved the construction of Currier in January 1908 and the building was put into use in the fall of 1909.

167

STATEMENT OF THE BOARD OF
TRUSTEES
June 30, 1962

To: All Alumni, Faculty and Undergraduates

A major issue, which has become increasingly serious and important during the past fifteen years, has come to the Board of Trustees for decision. The Board wishes to share this concern with every Williams alumnus and undergraduate.

The Committee on Review of Fraternity Questions submitted its Report at the end of the May meeting and it was considered by the Board on June 8, 9 & 10.

After extensive discussions the Board found itself in agreement that the fraternity, as the "fraternity" known to previous generations, has in fact ceased to exist on the Williams campus. It recognizes that at present fraternities are different in kind and play an entirely different role than in an earlier era. The Board further believes that the Report is correct in its essential analysis of the history and long-term evolution of the fraternity system on campuses such as ours and in its conclusion that provision of housing, eating, and social accommodations is properly a responsibility of the college.

The Board does not, however, wish to move hastily or arbitrarily in an area of long history, and deep attachments, for the fraternities have made a significant contribution to the life of the college. The Board urges that they review their relation to the college in the light of the Committee Report. The Board wishes to invite initiative on the part of the several fraternities and to remain responsive to conditions and circumstances as they may develop voluntarily or through negotiation.

The Board recognizes that many factors relating to physical plant and finances are involved which require detailed study. Among these are questions of alterations to existing plant, new construction, whether fraternity owned properties may become available to the college and estimates of the costs involved.

In order to assemble information required for decision, the Board voted (1) to direct the Secretary to have a copy of this statement and of the Committee's Report sent to every alumnus and all faculty and undergraduates, (2) to have meetings arranged between alumni and undergraduate representatives of each fraternity chapter and a group comprising representatives of the Board, the Administration and the Committee, (3) to appoint a Standing Committee to develop preliminary proposals and (4) to direct the Treasurer to prepare, in cooperation with the Standing Committee, estimates of financing requirements which such proposals would involve.

In the meantime the Board recommends that the Administration, Faculty and undergraduates join in cooperative efforts towards the fullest realization of the educational opportunities emphasized in the Report.

It is hoped that the Report, based on a long and thoughtful study, will be read with care by all alumni, for it is the unanimous judgment of a representative and devoted group of Williams men concerned with serving the educational purposes of the College.

Any communications relating to this Report or this Statement should be directed to the Secretary of the Board until such time as the Standing Committee is announced.

REPORT OF THE COMMITTEE ON REVIEW OF FRATERNITY QUESTIONS

To the President and Trustees of Williams College:~

This is the report of the committee of eleven Williams men constituted by you in October of 1961 to examine into the current fraternity situation at the College and make recommendations relative thereto. Of the eleven, two are undergraduates and nine are alumni. Two are Trustees and two are former Trustees. Ten of the eleven are members of a fraternity.

COMMITTEE PROCEDURE

In addition to work done individually or in groups by its members, the committee has held eight meetings. During the course of these meetings about thirty persons, some on invitation and others at their own request, have appeared before the committee to present their views as to the nature of existing problems related to the fraternity situation, as to facts and causes underlying these problems and as to suggested solutions. Those who thus gave assistance came from the undergraduate body, the alumni, and the faculty. They represented great diversity of opinion. A joint meeting was held with the Graduate Committee of Social Units of Williams College, at which alumni representatives of each of the fifteen fraternities now in existence at the College were heard.

Through the columns of the Alumni Review and of the Record, the committee invited statements from all members of the Williams family. A large number of such presentations were made, either in the form of letters (over fifty) or as formal statements of individuals or of groups.

In addition to the two student petitions of 1961 and the earlier letter circularized by an alumnus, the committee studied the reports of predecessor committees on the subject, particularly those of the Shriver Committee in 1945 and the Sterling Committee in 1951. Through its own personnel it also made certain factual studies, including the corresponding situation at a number of Eastern colleges.

PART I
CONCLUSION AND RECOMMENDATIONS

The committee, in consequence of the testimony given to it and as a result of its own deliberations, has unanimously arrived at the following conclusions and recommendations.

CONCLUSIONS:

1. Fraternities at Williams have come to exercise a disproportionate role in undergraduate life, and as a result the primary educational purposes of the College are not being fully realized.

2. Long continued delegation to the fraternities by the College of a large part of its responsibility with respect to the housing, eating, and social accommodations of the student body is a major cause of many existing conditions which are harmful to the educational purpose of the College; and early steps should be taken by the College to re-assume this responsibility and integrate these functions into the life of the College, where they properly belong.

RECOMMENDATIONS:

1. That the President and the Board of Trustees adopt and announce a firm policy to assume, at the earliest feasible date, complete responsibility for providing housing, eating, and social

accommodations for the entire student body in units owned and operated by the College.

2. That in furtherance of such policy the President and Trustees create a standing committee, based in Williamstown, and authorize such committee to propose plans, both general and specific, to implement the policy.

3. That such plans be directed not only toward full implementation of the policy at the earliest feasible date but also toward current actions which will serve as consistent affirmative and irreversible steps toward the early realization of the ultimate goal.

4. That in the formulation of plans for the creation of new College owned and operated units consideration be given to the use of existing as well as any necessary new physical facilities that may be required to implement the policy.

5. That the President and Treasurer of the College be given all necessary authority to negotiate with any fraternity which may wish to transfer its physical property to the College, whether by sale, exchange, gift, or other suitable method.

6. That the fraternities, except to the extent that their activities are reduced by reason of steps taken in furtherance of the policy, be allowed to continue to function with maximum freedom, subject to the present ban on discriminatory clauses in their own constitutions and in conformity with appropriate standards of safety and conduct to be set by the College.

7. That at an appropriate time the Williams family be advised as to the reasons for and merits of the above recommendations.

Hereinafter in Part II are recited the considerations which led your committee to the conclusions and recommendations above set forth.

PART II
THE COLLEGE PURPOSE

A liberal arts college should provide a total educational experience in which a deeply interested group of students are given maximum opportunity to make real progress, by constant exposure to diversity and challenge, toward understanding themselves and the world. That educational experience should play a vital role in helping the student to achieve, for himself, a character in which are deeply embedded all the better qualities. A college has a very short time in which to assist its young students toward such objectives and effect the transfer from the shelter of pre-college life to a realization of the problems involved in taking one's place in the world.

A small college, and particularly one able to sustain relatively high cost per student, should have advantages in such an endeavor because of its ability to organize a substantial part of the total educational experience around relatively small units where there can be a blending of classroom life and a life of conversation and discussion, together with opportunity to find and enjoy the values, disciplines, and pleasures of small-unit living, eating, and social life. These advantages should be available to all students.

Williams is a small college and has decided to remain so regardless of the pressures of the times. There is and will always be a real opportunity for smallness, derived from its excellence. There is a place for Williams as an example of smallness at its best if the years spent there represent a maximum exposure to all the facets of the educational process within a social framework that contributes to this result.

In its investigation, the committee's chief concern has been the educational process at Williams, a process not limited to classroom, laboratory and library, but including every possible stimulus and opportunity for creative and critical thinking and the development of sound individual values. Because of its small size, outstanding faculty and talented and diverse student body, Williams has the potential to offer to its students a total

173

educational experience unusual among higher educational institutions. The ability of the College to maintain its position as a first rate educational institution and to continue to attract the highest possible caliber of students and faculty will depend largely upon whether its unique potential can be fully realized. In a world where the fundamental values inherent in our nation and College face immediate, stark challenge on every side, Williams can do no less than provide a social framework that will advance its educational goals in the most effective way possible. The existing fraternity system must be evaluated in terms of its effect upon the attainment of this end.

HISTORY OF FRATERNITIES AT WILLIAMS

The first fraternity was established on the Williams campus in the year 1833. By 1850 there were six and by 1900 as many more. Gradually the fraternities gained acceptance as an integral part of the Williams scene and over the years a sizeable portion of the responsibility of the College was in effect delegated to them and has since remained largely in their hands. Of such nature are the housing of a considerable portion of the student body, the feeding of an even larger number, and numerous areas of student government, discipline, and social life. By and large the fraternities have handled these responsibilities well.

The inherent defect in the arrangements lay in the abdication by the College of part of its own responsibility and the resulting inability of the College to insure that non-academic aspects of student life contribute effectively to the educational process. For such time as the joint efforts by the College and by the fraternities remain in proper balance to achieve the desired result and generated only minor friction, the divided jurisdiction worked well. But the College had, by moving out of a large and important area of its own sovereignty, placed itself in a vulnerable position where it lacked facilities of its own with which to fill such void as might develop.

In the last few decades the handwriting of impending trouble has become increasingly visible on the Williams wall and countless hours have been spent by earnest alumni and students in attempts to ameliorate the situation. Non-fraternity men grew understandably restive at being excluded from the large area of Williams life centered in fraternities. To provide what seemed to be the best antidote available under the existing circumstances, the Commons Club, later known as the Garfield Club, was created. It failed of its purpose, largely because of the resentment felt by its members at being segregated in a group the very existence of which suggested their lack of acceptability as fraternity material.

Next followed the construction of Baxter Hall, with outstanding facilities open to all, and the removal of the Freshman class from all fraternity involvement. The new arrangements cut deeply into the budgets of the fraternities. Partly as a result of this economic pressure to increase membership, partly out of sympathy for those rejected, and partly because of a growing undergraduate feeling that the rigors and humiliations of the caste system had no useful place in the years of college life, fraternity doors opened ever more wide. Finally, as a not surprising culmination in this trend, the undergraduates evolved a rushing procedure known as "Total Opportunity", by virtue of which a man who agrees to accept whatever bid is offered to him is almost certain to receive one (though it may not correspond to his hopes and may not have been made with any enthusiasm on the part of the fraternity). As a matter of mechanics, this procedure has been successfully carried out for the last two years.

THE PRESENT SITUATION

Total Opportunity, like other prior attempts to correct inequities and imperfections in the complicated fraternity system, such as deferred rushing and the institution of a freshman dining hall, has alleviated certain conditions but has not solved the basic problem.

Many Williams men, undergraduates and alumni, both within and without the fraternities, find little appeal in fraternities as they are now constituted. They are intent on a new and better alignment wherein any student, with or without fraternity affiliation, may have equal opportunity with any of his fellows to find and enjoy the riches of four college years in pursuit of education and the rewards and satisfactions that go with it, without being hampered, distracted, or embarrassed in the process. These men feel that too much otherwise useful energy has already been wasted in wrestling with the fraternity problem and that the time has come to put an end to the pressure buildups that for so long and to so large an extent have monopolized the attention of many alumni and most of the undergraduates.

Testimony given to the committee indicates clearly that the fraternity system as it now functions is producing widespread dissatisfaction among all segments of the Williams family – the students, the faculty, the administration, and the alumni. Most of the faculty and a growing number of the students (including members of fraternities) feel that current fraternity life obstructs the educational purposes of the College and handicaps those intent on achieving the full benefit of these purposes. Many of the alumni believe that Total Opportunity has made a mockery of the original concept of fraternities as voluntary associations of like-minded people. The administrative officers of the College appear to lack effective means of control of student social life and discipline because of the quasi-sovereign nature of the fraternities. There is a growing demand, both by students and by alumni, for reasonable control over fraternity behavior, particularly as to Hell Week, public and private conduct and the use of alcohol. The isolation of the Freshmen from beneficial contacts with the rest of the College community is criticized on both social and intellectual grounds, although its value is recognized as to the promotion of class unity and initial concentration on College objectives. Insufficient opportunity is found for informal contact between students of all classes and faculty members. The Junior Adviser system is said to be weakened by the pressure of the present fraternity system. There is complaint that attractive applicants to

Williams are being lost because the College is too fraternity-oriented. The added cost of a Williams education resulting from fraternity dues and other fees is criticized. And, even under Total Opportunity, a considerable number are disturbed by the selection-rejection aspects of the present rushing process and its effect on the attitude of the students toward their College life. This is evidenced by the increasing stratification of the houses (whereby the strong become stronger and the weak become weaker), the lack of morale in many of them, the resulting handicaps on the serious minded student, and the acceptance of superficial and false values by those involved in the time consuming business of rushing – a striking repetition of a condition described over ten years ago in the Sterling Report: "The making of a fraternity becomes exaggerated beyond all proper proportion, and the academic functions of college assume a secondary role."

It would serve little purpose to attempt to recite the evidence in detail or to assess the relative importance of those various criticisms. It is enough to say that the committee has found them all valid in greater or lesser degree and that their cumulative weight is such that a change appears to be imperative. The committee believes that any further temporizing will only make matters worse and that the change to be made must be of a more basic nature than any previous efforts. Such former devices as quotas, moving rushing back to sophomore year, the establishment and demise of a "separate-but-equal" facility, the isolation of Freshmen, the creation of Baxter Hall, the banning of prejudice clauses in fraternity constitutions, and finally Total Opportunity itself, were all directed to the mechanics of how a long continued system could be made to operate better. But all too often these devices had the effect of further compounding the problem – an indication that its roots go deep. In the opinion of your committee, the key to a more basic approach is to be found in the fact that Williams College, which at present leaves to the fraternities the responsibility for feeding 94 percent of the three upper classes, for housing 44 percent of them, and for providing most of the social life for all of them, has thereby sacrificed its opportunity and foregone its duty to merge the academic and social aspects of the students' lives in a manner which would inevitably make the educational process easier of accomplishment and more complete. The fraternities, at the heart and center of the College, now play a role which is so all encompassing that their influence tends to interfere with the broader, more inclusive ends of the College itself.

THE REMEDY

The committee believes that the College should, as soon as may be, adopt and carry out a policy to provide College owned and operated housing, feeding, and social facilities for the entire student body. The practice at other educational institutions indicates that this suggestion is not as revolutionary as it might at first appear. Williams College is in no position to adopt a House Plan such as exists at Harvard and Yale nor does this seem the most creative solution for Williams. Instead, working with such tools as are available or can be made available, the College can go a long way in providing a set of facilities, partly new and partly converted, which would have great advantages over mass dining halls and colorless dormitories and provide a distinctive set of facilities for full enjoyment by the entire College body of the values of group living within the boundaries of the educational process.

It is realized that the recommended action will have a considerable impact on the fraternities, which have for so long been accustomed to consider the functions of housing, feeding, and social life as to a large extent their own functions of housing, feeding and social life as to a large extent their own responsibility and essential to their purpose. But the fraternities must of course give way to the College in any conflict of interest between them. If a move is to be made for the good of the College, the fraternities must be prepared to accommodate themselves to it, even though the readjustment be painful They, as well as all other entities, must bow to the paramount right and duty of the College to pursue the broadest objectives of a liberal arts education.

In arriving at its conclusions, the committee has not been unmindful of the positive and vital contributions that have been made by the fraternities to their members and to the College. They have earned the affection and loyalty of thousands of Williams men. Operating as small, closely-knit groups, they have provided for their members great opportunity for self-discipline, social adjustment, and the assumption of responsibility, from which many have benefited. The high ideals of their charters have been impressed upon many of their initiates and the relationships between alumni and undergraduates have been of mutual advantage. The memories of many alumni (including most of the committee) are nostalgic with respect to the pleasure and profits received from their fraternity association. But the fact still remains that the fraternities constitute a serious obstacle to the realization of the full educational potential of the College. This is becoming increasingly apparent.

The recommendation of the committee is a transfer of certain College activities back to the College, so that the fraternities will cease to be the focal point for eating, living, and social arrangements. The College will then be in a far stronger position to extend the educational process outside of the classroom and make it more effective. The fraternities could continue under such changed conditions. If they sought smaller quarters more suited to their reduced activities, the College should go a long way to make the transition as easy and painless as possible. In their new status, the fraternities could well have greater freedom than they now have in such areas as determining the nature and size of their membership and in their rushing and pre-rushing activities, provided their conduct and any outside affiliations are consistent with the policies of the College.

It is obvious that the proposed plan will take time. It is also obvious that the transition period will be a difficult one because, until the program is in full operation, existing divisions and rigidities on the campus may temporarily become even more serious. In consequence, it is important that the transition period be made as short as possible and that certain major steps in that transition be taken or made known with all possible speed by the President and the Board of Trustees.

The committee believes that wide support will be given to a firm course of action which clearly and irrevocably points the road that Williams intends to take and leaves to the Board, the Administration, and the wisdom of the fellowship of Williams men the question of the manner and timing in which the change shall be accomplished. The committee further believes that such action will enlist the active cooperation of all concerned in a common endeavor to build better for the future of the College, whatever the time, expense, and effort involved.

IMPLEMENTATION

Although the drawing of a blueprint or detailed suggestions for implementing the committee's recommendation is a matter beyond its province and should be left to others as the plan develops, it might not be amiss to record the present thinking of the committee as to methods which might be employed.

If ample funds were available and no problem existed as to full use of an existing college plant, the ideal way in which to carry out a plan for providing housing, eating, and social facilities for the entire student body of a small college such as Williams would be the building of a sufficient number of comparable units to perform these services for groups of perhaps one hundred each, whose non-classroom life would be focused in these units. Each unit would have its own dining hall operated by the College, its own housing accommodations, and its own quarters for social activity. It could also have its own limited library, especially in the field of largely attended courses. Since there would be no appreciable difference between the units, there would be no basis for condescension or envy, but there could well be an intense rivalry between the units in intramural matters. Each unit might contain representatives of all classes, giving to each class the full benefit of contact with other classes, and each unit should have a form of self-government within limits. Membership might be controlled to the extent necessary to assure that each unit would remain strong and diversified. There could be a healthy informal faculty participation, particularly at meals.

But obviously this ideal is impossible of immediate achievement, as ample funds are not at present available and not all of the existing buildings at Williams are designed to fit into such a pattern or susceptible of suitable adaptation.

Nonetheless, there could be almost immediate combinations of adjoining buildings, in order to get the plan started. Such combinations could result in the creation of what would amount to a "unit", with the housing accommodations in one building and the eating and social facilities in another, adjacent if possible. The dormitory now under construction might well be included with one of its neighbors in a unit of this nature.

At the same time, firm commitment should be made for the early construction of at least one and preferably two complete new units on sites such as the Greylock parcel. The cost of these would be considerable but it could be added to and absorbed in current plans for raising large funds needed for other purposes, without alienating the response and support of those who are always ready to meet a Williams need.

It may well develop that some fraternities, or a group of them, will decide to convey their existing properties to the College and acquire more modest facilities better adapted to their remaining functions. If so, adjacent fraternity houses, if acquired by the College, might be converted so that one house would in effect become a dormitory and the other a dining, social, and study facility.

The committee's recommendation that a standing committee be created to assist in carrying out the plans grows out of the realization that there will be many difficult and complex problems requiring more attention than can be given to them by the Board and deserving in certain instances the opinions of experts in the particular field. Some of such problems are apparent at present; others of real importance will arise as the plan progresses.

One of the first items to be considered should be that of consultation with each of the fraternities, in order to determine whether there may be a basis for negotiation as to the acquisition of its property. If there is, the College should be prepared, in view of their honorable record on the Williams campus and the ultimate economic readjustment involved in the new plan, to adopt as generous a policy as is possible. This policy should be continued in the future for such fraternities as may later decide to dispose of their present houses.

In dealing with the fraternities, as in dealing with the entire Williams family, the committee's recommendation as to disclosure of the considerations on which the plan is based is believed to be of considerable importance. The suggested course will seriously disturb many alumni who are deeply attached to their fraternities to which they have faithfully given of their time and substance over the years, as have most of the members of the committee. Sentiment will run strong for a preservation of the fraternities in the form which so many of us knew. But conditions have greatly altered.

The undergraduates and the younger alumni are as cognizant of the present situation as are the members of the committee but the older ones have in most cases no conception of how the campus climate has changed since they were a part of it. Some of the reasons for this change involve factors which are not confined to Williams, but, rather, result from basic changes in our society. Williamstown is less isolated and fraternities no longer perform the unique functions they once did. The academic demands made upon students have become far greater, and the interest of students in graduate work requiring good academic records has caused a decided shift in interest. It is believed that full and open disclosure of the present situation would result in general acceptance of the proposed plan, without bitterness or hostility. Williams men are more intent on the good of Williams than on their own preferences derived from a mode of living which has to a very great extent faded into history. We are confident that when the Williams alumni are presented with the facts, they will not only accept the steps which the College decides are necessary, but they will also set to work on the challenging task of making the new program an outstanding success.

THE FUTURE

It is the belief of the committee that the plan herein presented would constitute a truly exciting development in the history of Williams College. It would create a campus where education, in its broadest sense, would take place everywhere and at all times and where constant and unhampered exchange of ideas between the faculty and students of differing background and experience would become the norm of College life and the best possible preparation for the challenges of tomorrow. It is not designed to make a bad Williams good, but to make a good Williams better.

Respectfully submitted by

The Committee

Jay B. Angevine '11, Chairman
John S. Osborne '25
Ferdinand K. Thun '30
Edward L. Stanley '37
William B. Gates, Jr. '39
Frederic S. Nathan '43
M. Michael Griggs '44
Dickinson R. Debevoise '46
Robert J. Geniesse '51
Robert J. Durham, Jr. '62
Bruce D. Grinnell '62
J. Hodge Markgraf '52, Secretary

May 5, 1962

PLANS AND PURPOSES
A Preliminary Report of the President

Fellow Alumni and Friends of the College:

As we come to the close of a busy year, I have been urged to report to all in writing what I have been able to discuss in person with many of you, at gatherings in Williamstown and elsewhere, about the course and purpose of Williams College.

That this has been an active year is apparent to all who have followed events on the campus. Much of the discussion and information sent to alumni in the last year has, of necessity, dealt with the problem of making an orderly transition from one residential system to another. Yet this change is only one aspect of a larger and more comprehensive program for the future which has been developing here for a year and half. While the written word is not a substitute for direct discussion and observation on the scene, I would like to send you this preliminary report and invite you to explore those ideas further on your visits here.

The physical changes which have taken place on the campus some of you have seen: the cover on the hockey rink which has made possible extended intercollegiate and intra- mural hockey as well as skating for all age- groups including faculty and an enthusiastic children's league; the completing of the first new dormitory Williams has built since Lehman Hall in 1927, and one greatly appreciated by its new occupants; the moving of the oldest college observatory in America to its third and we trust final resting place - and its restoration for a whole new life of usefulness with the dedication on May 4, 1963, of the Willis I. Milham planetarium, utilizing the interior dome which Professor Albert Hopkins and his students built in 1837; the addition to the Library to provide space for the Roper Center of Public Opinion Research with faculty offices on the floors above; the relocation of the over- crowded Admissions Office and Deans' and Registrar's

Offices in Hopkins; the subdivision of Goodrich Hall to provide new classrooms; and finally the building of a new Service Building opposite Weston Field to bring together maintenance operations that had been scattered at considerable cost over seven different locations. These changes are now in being and I hope you will enjoy seeing them on your return.

Some of these improvements and others to come are being coordinated with the advice of professional assistance in campus planning, to help us insure a well-thought-out program for the location of activities, the flows of people, the placing of new facilities, and the comprehensive development of the campus. Preliminary proposals suggest the location of a new residential complex on the Greylock corner in lieu of the two separate dormitories previously considered to meet our needs, and the possible diversion of traffic from in front of the Library to create a new and natural quadrangle bounded by Chapin, Lehman and Stetson Library. Other plans, as have been earlier indicated, would so locate a language center, a public affairs center and other academic activities on the central and western end of the campus as to allow a closer relation of residential and educational life.

But a college is far more than its physical plant. It is the sum of the history and objectives, the people and programs that enter into its continuing purposes -the pursuit of truth, the diffusion of knowledge, and the growth of young men as able, thoughtful and responsible contributors to their several callings.

To serve these continuing goals under rapidly changing conditions has required all first-class institutions of higher education to re-examine both what they do and how best they can do it. In this task we have fortunately been aided by an unrestricted grant of $50,000 from the Carnegie Corporation to assist the work of forward planning. A number of faculty and administrative personnel have accordingly been at work, in consultation with the Trustees, investigating many aspects of the College, recording progress made in recent years, and suggesting objectives and programs for the next decade.

I

There are three basic characteristics of Williams from which we begin and in which we can take pride. It is, first of all, a strong teaching institution which can properly point to the quality of its faculty in the basic fields of learning -their training, dedication and interest in teaching undergraduates. With most of the faculty living within five minutes of the campus, student-faculty relationships are meaningful and offer still further possibilities ahead. Despite the relative isolation of Williamstown, good men come here and stay because of the attractions of the college and the community and the quality of the undergraduates with whom they have the opportunity to work and whom they can come to know as individuals, not only in the classroom but outside as well.

A second outstanding characteristic is the devotion to the liberal arts ideal that exists on the Williams campus. This is more than a shibboleth here. We are small enough so that faculty members can know each other and are not confined to colleagues or conversation in their own fields. In an age of increasing specialization this awareness of each other's work and interests has brought an appreciation of excellence across professional lines. This reflects itself in a feeling on the part of almost all of the faculty that students should be encouraged to work both within and beyond the different professional fields - that they should seek a broad- ranging education.   Herein lies one reason why a science major at Williams typically takes more courses outside his division than within it; why two thirds of our students take at least one course in the History of Art, although none is required; and why more than half of our premedical candidates major in fields other than the sciences.

A third basic strength is the impressive range of talents and aspirations of the students who come here and the opportunities that this kind of residential college can offer them in the years ahead. These already extend beyond the usual curricular offerings and the formal and informal athletic and other extracurricular activities of a diverse and lively student body, to further relationships that a small college in a small town allows. In addition to those serving as teaching assistants at the College, approximately fifty undergraduates have taught at the Mount Greylock Regional School, and others are involved in tutoring projects in North Adams and elsewhere. The Berkshire Symphony Orchestra numbers fifteen Williams men among its regular members. Students participate regularly in the work of local churches, the Boys' Club, the Berkshire Farm School (a rehabilitation center for boys), and volunteer efforts of other kinds.

These situations add a dimension of contact with reality that can enlarge and deepen the lives of young men. Nor would many Williams men underestimate the meaning and value of spending four years in this kind of magnificent setting in the pattern of lives largely spent in urban environments.

II

From these three basic characteristics examination has naturally turned to the core of any educational institution - its curriculum. As one looks back at the academic program at Williams over the last decade, one finds that major revisions have been few. Although changes have been substantial elsewhere, the feeling here has been that the balance in course offerings between "distribution" and "concentration" has stood up at least as well as most of the alternatives suggested. Students are still required to take two courses in each of the three major areas of liberal learning; i.e., the humanities, the social sciences, and the natural sciences. The "major sequence" of courses leads to a double-credit senior course and a comprehensive examination in the major field.

With the stream of better-prepared students coming to us, and with the higher motivation in a student body of whom approximately seventy per cent now go on to graduate schools, there has been a steady increase in the number of undergraduates seeking a degree with honors. Inherent in the continuing growth of the honors program is the increasing ability and desire of our undergraduates to do more independent work and to explore more on their own in their fields of interest. The faculty is currently studying ways to bring about a more flexible curriculum, more responsive to the opportunities ahead, with a possible relaxation of certain formal quantitative requirements. The change in the residential system, designed to open up the campus as a more effective educational community, will encourage this trend.

The explosion of knowledge in all fields, plus the changing interests of students and the opportunities before them, have this year brought two new majors into being, Astrophysics and Religion; and there is mounting demand for a major in Russian which we will offer as soon as resources allow.

Perhaps nowhere can the present generation's expanding interest in the larger world be better exemplified than in the current program to add to our course offerings in Area Studies. A few years ago our curriculum offered more than ninety courses on Europe and North America and only three on the rest of the world, a distribution which no longer corresponds with the world that young men of today are going to have to face in the course of lives reaching well into the next century. We are accordingly adding new courses in Latin American, Russian, African, Near and Far Eastern affairs in a program which will relate these new courses to existing departments of instruction. The fundamental objective of the Area Studies program at Williams is at once to enable undergraduates to study civilizations outside of the Western world and to sharpen their understanding of their own culture by studying another.

Our current program draws on the experience and talents of present faculty members. The needs for the future appear to be financial resources to permit present faculty members to deepen their backgrounds in particular geographical areas and to provide for additional faculty members with area strengths, particularly in foreign languages, and for work in anthropology.

In this connection the Graduate Center for the Study of Development Economics at Cluett House deserves note. This Ford Foundation- sponsored project brings twenty men ⸗

government leaders, bankers, businessmen from underdeveloped nations all over the globe to Williamstown each year for a concentrated program leading to a Master's Degree in Development Economics. Its presence here has given the Departments of Economics and Political Science a great stimulus, and an emphasis on overseas research and applied work which is probably unique among small colleges. Every senior member of the Economics staff brings to his classes the direct experience of time spent abroad, teaching, doing research, or advising foreign projects or governments. By careful planning such first-hand contacts with developments overseas as well as at home are expected to continue.

III

Another program, which has come forward during this period of evaluation and planning, relates to a new and exciting conception on this campus for the teaching of science, particularly in the honors program. Basically this idea, developed by our younger scientists and reviewed and approved by their seniors, involves greater student participation in the process of research as a teaching method. Qualified students will be actively involved in research with a teaching faculty member, thereby making possible a closer realization of the "Mark Hopkins and the log" ideal than has been possible here in the sciences. Already faculty-student research teams are working in solid state and laser physics, on mechanisms of organic reactions in chemistry, and other projects in biology, psychology and geology. To implement this plan fully would call for a carefully planned grouping of the new science facilities needed to supplement the venerable Thompson Laboratories. The logical location for such a new science center would be the west end of the Lab Campus. In it would be placed needed small laboratories and a central core of instruments, common to more than one field, which a college the size of Williams could not wisely attempt to duplicate in each department.

An important feature of the building will be its interdisciplinary character whereby faculty and students, in this age of greater and greater specialization, will be made more aware of the problems and techniques of adjacent fields of learning. Just as graduate schools have been moving toward departments of biophysics, physical chemistry, etc., this new facility will permit a natural cross-fertilization between allied fields. So favorable has been the response to what we feel is a unique addition to undergraduate liberal arts teaching in the sciences that we have just received a small foundation grant to proceed with its systematic planning.

For many years we have also had close and constructive working relations with two research industries located in our neighborhood. We assist them professionally and arrange an M.A. or M.S. program for their younger scientists, and they in turn have helped both in our laboratory and section teaching and in other kinds of support of the College. The proposed new science center will encourage more relationships of this kind. It will also foster the kind of summer programs through which Williams can further contribute to the training of teachers for the nation's schools.

In addition to these programs, we plan to continue to capitalize on particular "shafts of strength" available to this College. Among these are the Roper Center of Public Opinion Research, the largest collection of public opinion data in the world. Beyond its availability to students and faculty here, it brings a stream of distinguished scholars to the campus and has added a new dimension to our work.

A similar opportunity lies in the field of art, where the arrival in Williamstown of the exceptional Clark Art Institute has provided the significant possibility of combining a strong college art department with the Clark's remarkable collection and expanding facilities to create a new kind of art center. This might usefully be directed to the training of teachers for secondary schools and liberal arts colleges (below the Ph.D. level), with a course of study emphasizing creative teaching in a field of rising interest at all levels of education.

Allied to this is the need to remain responsive to the new possibilities of audio-visual techniques of instruction, a frontier of rapid development calling for careful study. It already points toward a new language center and other possibilities beyond that either might be attached to the Library or to the Theater, or possibly best located in one of the present fraternity buildings.

IV

The spread of extracurricular opportunities greatly enriches today's over-all college experience. Athletics, as attested by the records of recent teams, continue to play an important part in the educational process at Williams. Under the pressures of current academic demands, participation in sports contributes a critical stretch and balance and change of pace to the total program. Long-run plans point to certain additions to athletic facilities, though I doubt that we will ever be able to accommodate all the wide-ranging interests of undergraduates. Last spring I discovered that intercollegiate contests were being held here in long-distance bike racing, motorcycling, rugby, white-water canoeing and judo - in addition to regularly organized sports - and I understand that a parachute club has been formed recently. This, too, gives an example of the range and vitality of the students who are coming to this kind of college.

As part of our resolve to maintain the constructive and attractive features of small group living traditional at Williams, we plan to lend all practical support to the active intramural program which our setting encourages and which adds relaxation and humor as well as recreation to a busy program.

I have elsewhere spoken and written on the admissions question, as has Fred Copeland, indicating both the potentials and the problems inherent in the rising tide of applications—this year the highest we have ever had.

Because we all know that present tests and grading systems do not adequately measure some of the most important qualities in the long-run growth of human beings - including intellectual growth - we have this year initiated the modest program announced earlier of accepting at least ten per cent of each class on the basis of recommendations of exceptional gifts or personal promise that exceeds strict academic performance. This has been reported to you before, but you should know that this program, helpfully underwritten by a grant from the Ford Foundation, has been sent to more than 2,000 schools with the express purpose of encouraging them to recommend students to us who might otherwise be discouraged from applying and whose unusual strengths, talents, or potentials for leadership we want at Williams. Needless to say - in a category that is heavily over-subscribed - we will seek to admit only those who can handle the work here, but we want to keep open more doors than one under the pressures that lie ahead.

We also hope to develop a new chapter in the College's relation to its alumni, carrying further for those who wish it the kind of continuing educational relationship foreshadowed in the June Alumni Seminars and the Summer Program in American Studies for Executives.

VI

The massive changes bearing upon higher education today - from above and below in education itself, as well as laterally from an expanding society - have led to forebodings in some quarters about the future of the independent liberal arts college. The problems are serious enough to have urged intensive self - examination upon us all. I hope these brief remarks have indicated some of the kinds of studies we have been undertaking here.

Yet I have no doubt of the fundamental validity of the enterprise itself. Provided it plans wisely and its urgent financial problems can be solved, the case for the liberal arts college has perhaps never been stronger. Fifteen years of teaching as a member of the faculty of two great universities has impressed me with their power, research and resources, and at the same time heightened my sense of the complementary role that remains for the independent liberal arts college.

While at Williams this starts from and centers on its conscious teaching tradition—its focus on gifted teaching of important subjects for able, varied, and inquiring undergraduates—it can no longer stop with this fundamental. We must adapt what we do to the better preparation and increasing ability levels of our students, building on and anticipating the greater depth and quality demands of their prior and subsequent education. We may also have to add particular reinforcing strengths to meet new developments. But above all we have the controlling responsibility, and a special opportunity, to go beyond good instruction in particular fields. We can seek to maintain the balance of the liberal arts college experience. Both within their formal education and beyond, we can try to equip young men not just to bridge such cleavages in the culture as C. P. Snow has emphasized, but to develop what William James called the "critical sense," to discover routes to various kinds of understanding, to be concerned with the potentialities of knowledge and the character and purposes of those who use it.

In the twenty-year sequence of education that most of our students now undergo, the college years frequently offer their first chance, and for many the only real chance, to stand up and look around on their own at ideas, at their world, at themselves. None of us can now foresee the problems that they will have to comprehend and cope with in the year 2000. The best we can do is to try to develop their capacity to see and think and feel, to question, to weigh, to judge and to act; their insight into the ways of thought and the qualities of men and ideas that make the difference.

To take advantage of this opportunity, and to justify limiting our size in the face of increasing numbers and rising costs, Williams must develop to the full its potentials as a residential liberal arts college. The presence of 1200 able students, a faculty of 120, and a wide variety of interesting residents, alumni and other visitors working as an educational community in a setting of this kind, offers opportunities that have yet to be fully realized. Opening up internal barriers, bringing freshmen back into unrestricted contact with the college, relocating and

193

recombining educational and residential activities, moving toward more flexible curricular arrangements, encouraging individual inquiry and responsibility, linking formal study to informal discussion and to extracurricular possibilities—these and other distinctive potentials allow a remarkable kind of future growth for Williams as a residential liberal arts college under the conditions ahead.

America, as a civilization, will not perish from lack of specialized knowledge or specialized institutions. Its greatest need may rather be the development of men of larger understanding and of the qualities and judgment to assume its complex burdens. For this purpose the first-class liberal arts college, itself a unique creation of the American scene, remains a notable and most promising institution. As I understand it, such is the central purpose to which Williams is dedicated.

John E. Sawyer
May 28, 1963

WILLIAMS ALUMNI ACTION COMMITTEE

P.O. Box 1929
Grand Central Station
New York 17, New York

June 7, 1963

Fellow Alumnus:

Since our last letter to you as an alumnus who was interested enough to register opposition to the Angevine manifesto and its immediate implementation without further study, much has transpired. The trustees and administration have been moving as "hastily and arbitrarily in an area of long history and deep attachments" as they possibly can, contrary to their June 10, 1962, representation that they did not wish to do so. We thought It would be appropriate at this time to bring you up-to-date on what has transpired since our last communication to you and give you such information as may not have appeared in the Spring issue of the Williams Newsletter and May issue of the Williams Alumni Review.

Only 139 applications have been received for 144 places in the two new residential units which will occupy Berkshire Hall, the new dormitory and the new dining complex currently under construction. Of the 139, 43 are currently freshmen. The freshmen class has not been convinced that the proposed program will provide the freedom, responsibility and individuality which the fraternities have always had. The fraternity cause has been well presented by pro-fraternity undergraduates. The figures prove the success of their efforts.

The president of the Kappa Alpha alumni, in a letter to The Williams Record which appeared in its March 22 issue, pointed out that its offer to donate its house "was contingent upon the adoption of a comprehensive program whereby all undergraduates will be obliged to live and eat in facilities provided by Williams College. Consequently, the gift would not take effect until the adoption of a program applicable to all Williams fraternities."

The board of trustees of Beta Theta Pi adopted four resolutions on March 6, 1963:

1. We will not under present circumstances turn the chapter house over to the College.

2. We respectfully believe that fraternities, and especially this fraternity, do have and can continue to have a proper place in the Williams College life, and, with proper guidance, are capable of positive contributions to the advancement of the educational ideals to which Williams College is dedicated.

3. We shall join with other college groups in urging and prompting a rational, constructive, and workable solution to the social, intellectual, and academic problems we now face.

4. We shall support our undergraduate chapter in working toward such a solution.

The president of the Theta Delta Chi Association of Williams College wrote the following letter to The Record, which appeared in the May 3 issue:

"As president of the Theta Delta Chi Association of Williams College and a member of its Board of Trustees, I feel that it is important to make our position on the future of our fraternity clear to all concerned, for many years our Trustees have seen a real deficiency in the Williams social system, in that it did not provide a decent alternative to the fraternities. We are now genuinely pleased with the availability of the social units and even though they are too late arriving on the scene, we wish them the very best of luck. As a measure of their strength, we note that the new units were chosen by a number of fraternity members, including some outstanding men from Theta Delta Chi; we feel that these actions, based upon conviction, foreshadow an excellent turn of events.

"We have recently been led to understand that a number of the present fraternities are making plans to become social units, either before or shortly after the beginning of the forthcoming fall term. We have heard that a few houses even intend to discontinue their existence on the campus. Because of these semi-announced plans and the possible resulting confusion, we feel it is desirable for the TDX Association to make its position and policy clear.

"The Theta Delta Chi trustees, on April 20, 1963, voted to continue Theta Delta Chi on the campus as a fraternity and to continue the fraternity in our own facilities on Park Street. We have carefully reviewed the college's plans for us to sponsor a social unit, and we have decided against it. We can provide the same guarantees to our TDX undergraduates of continued use of the facilities, while at the same time continuing a real fraternity with what that implies. One measure of the guarantee which we intend to provide, is that we will subsidize our undergraduates on their room and board bills, so that we will remain competitive financially.

"We believe that there will be a place on the campus for fraternities whose members find some enjoyment and benefit in their voluntary association. It is our intent to provide to the undergraduate an opportunity for this association by remaining at Williams in our present location for as long as a practical need and desire exists."

The trustees of the Zeta Psi Fraternity in Williams College were served with a show cause order by the Zeta Psi Fraternity of North America on April 29, staying action by the trustees with regard to the leasing, selling, turning over or surrendering their real estate and improvements to Williams College until determination of this action by the Supreme Court of New York. On May 1 counsel answered the order, and May 9 was set as hearing day for the opposing briefs. The case has subsequently been given to a referee for additional study, and the next hearing will be on June

197

7. Meanwhile, the trustees are enjoined from taking any action on the property.

The trustees of Sigma Phi announced they have voted to lease its property to the college on a three-year basis and to sponsor a residential unit in the fall of 1963. The terms of the lease will be subject to the approval of the alumni of the Williams Chapter of Sigma Phi. If the alumni disapprove of the trustees' action, the lease will not be executed. The Sigma Phi undergraduates themselves disapprove of the proposal and would prefer to retain the status quo as a fraternity, according to The Record. Sigma Phi will remain at Williams.

Delta Kappa Epsilon trustees voted to recommend to its membership at the annual meeting June 15 that the chapter house be leased to the College for three years, so that it can be used in planning for the new residential system proposed for the campus.

Chi Psi's board of governors voted to sponsor a residential unit in the fall of 1963, pending approval by the alumni body as a whole. The property it owns will be leased to the college for four years. The undergraduate chapter will become dormant.

The other eight fraternities have not announced their positions as yet. It is known that some have adopted a "wait-and-see" policy and plan to watch carefully how the two trial residential units function in competition with the fraternities.

The question of legality has arisen in several instances. Some national fraternities feel that leasing or selling a chapter house would be grounds for revocation or suspension of a chapter's charter, and all records and property, including the chapter house, would revert to the national fraternity under the provisions of the constitution. An argument which has been advanced is that, in the event of a lease or sale to the college, the national fraternity would be deprived of its property without just compensation and without due process of law.

A second argument is that selling or leasing the property is directly contrary to the purpose for which some corporations were organized, and consequently the legality of the action is subject to very serious question. The corporation might be enjoined, and there also arises the question of the liability of the trustees (or governors or directors) to any members who do not consent to the transfer.

Williams has fallen far behind Amherst and Wesleyan in the last 50 years in the matter of endowment. Amherst's endowment stands today at $69,000,000; Wesleyan's at $54,000,000; Williams' at $42,000,000. Williams has been making a detailed study of its long-range educational program since 1961 and has engaged the firm of Marts & Lundy, Inc., campaign directors, which has made many surveys preparatory to fund raising campaigns, to make a study for Williams and to recommend the proper procedure for the execution of its program. Best estimates indicate that Williams will require an additional $25,000,000 for endowment, plant and contingencies over the next ten years. However, it is doubtful that the climate at present is conducive to fund raising among many, and perhaps the great majority of, Williams alumni.

President Sawyer has stated that, as the college's chief administration officer, he has been instructed by the trustees of the college to get on with the matter of implementation. He has undertaken a gruelling series of speaking engagements to sway sentiment for implementation among various alumni groups throughout the country. The trustees have approved the appointment of a provost, which position will involve the economic policies of the college, thus freeing the president from some of his administrative chores to pursue this assignment.

Most members of our committee have heard President Sawyer's speech on the present and future social structure. It is very

199

polished, but highly unconvincing. Whenever students are asked to attend meetings where alumni are present, such as at the recent Gargoyle Alumni meeting in New York, and on other occasions, whether in Williamstown or outside, it would seem that they are carefully screened for their pro-Angevine leanings. It is rare that an alumnus gets the opportunity to talk with pro-fraternity under-graduates at any Williams alumni function, even though pro-fraternity undergraduates are in the vast majority.

Consequently it is understandable that the students are beginning to believe in the inevitability of the proposed system. The Graduate Committee of Williams College Social Units, which consists of the presidents of alumni corporations or their designated representatives and alternates, has been completely ineffective because of its lack of unanimity.

During the spring vacation of the college, alumni committee members from a select group of six fraternities (Chi Psi, DKE, Phi Delta Theta, Zeta Psi, Kappa Alpha and Sigma Phi) were invited by the administration to meet in Williamstown with the trustees' committee of Messrs. Banks, Driscoll, Flynt, Foehl and Sawyer. Some of these houses had indicated that they preferred group action by several houses to individual action, and the trustees' committee provided the forum for these houses. On April 17 the Graduate Committee listened to a report of this meeting (and of a subsequent meeting in New York on April 15 of the same houses plus Alpha Delta Phi). The report revealed, among other things that, if a fraternity elected to continue, as it might under the original interpretation of the Angevine manifesto, the administration strongly favored that it conduct its operations in college - owned, rather than in privately - owned facilities. Further it was stated that fraternities electing to continue at Williams would probably have to share college - owned facilities with other fraternities, but each would have separate quarters.

It is unfortunate that the Graduate Committee has drifted and temporized. Positive and early action by it might have rendered orderly the present vertigo of events. Even now, if a majority of the houses were to show any fight and state that they still want a deferral of implementation to see how the experimental units work out; or if a majority were to state that unless their request for a delay is granted, they will recommend to their members that they refuse to contribute to the college as long as deferral is refused - then results might be forthcoming. Since the Graduate Committee, a constituted group, has given no leadership, the Action Committee can only recommend that the individual members of the Society of Alumni take some action at the June 15 meeting. We believe that if the administration and trustees are confronted with the refusal of the majority of the fraternities to sell, lease or give their houses to the college, or if the alumni show determined opposition to the Angevine Plan at the meeting on June 15, the trustees will be forced to modify their position and give the alumni a chance to plead their case.

The reunion program for June 15 calls for the annual meeting of the Society of Alumni at 11:00 a.m. in Chapin Hall. This meeting will have elections and various reports and will endeavor to postpone any motions of a controversial nature. Since President Sawyer is scheduled to speak at 2:30 p.m. on "Long-Range Plans for Williams" in Jesup Hall, we feel certain that controversial questions will be referred to the later meeting. If the alumni have any desire to take any action, it would be well to adjourn the morning meeting and to reconvene it after President Sawyer's talk, when there would be sufficient time for a thorough discussion of his plans by the duly constituted alumni body.

It has also been suggested that Edward L. Stanley '37, who will be nominated for the presidency of the Society of Alumni, should disqualify himself as the presiding officer at the June 15 meeting when the Angevine Report will be discussed, and permit the chair to be occupied by an alumnus whose mind is open.

You and 2500 other alumni have been interested enough in the deplorable situation at Williams to send in a check or at least a vote. You now have two opportunities to make your views count - (a) to vote at your fraternity meeting not to sell, lease or give your house to the college and to urge all your friends to do likewise, and (b) to come to the alumni meeting on June 15 and vote for deferral of the Angevine Plan so that the trustees' "hasty and arbitrary" action can be discussed and possibly modified.

Respectfully submitted,

WILLIAMS ALUMNI ACTION COMMITTEE (consisting of
373 Alumni of Williams College)

By: The Executive Committee

SUMNER FORD '08	JEROME W. BRUSH, JR. '39
HENRY R. JOHNSTON '09	PAUL M. AUBRY '40
EWART G. DAVIES '12	CHARLES M. WILDS '40
ROLAND PALMEDO '17	HUBERT R. HUDSON '49

STOCKTON D. FISHER '33

ACKNOWLEDGEMENTS

AND

SOUCRCES

The information in this book draws upon a variety of published materials; dozens of exchanges by letter and email; and hundreds of conversations with Williams alumni, administrative officers, students, faculty, and trustees over a period of almost sixty years, but especially over the past two years. Many who aided me are listed here, but undoubtedly I have overlooked some who deserve mention. I cannot overstate the gratitude, admiration, and affection I feel for all the colleagues and friends who have helped me in chronicling this story that we shared and lived in varying ways.

Conversations with Anne Sawyer and her recorded interview with Charles Alberti '51 provided information and insights that were both valuable and not available from other sources. Communications with all four Sawyer children—Katherine, John, Stephen, and William—also were of great assistance. I learned much from the senior honors thesis by President Sawyer's grandson, Robinson Sawyer '03, "The Elimination of Fraternities at Williams College" (2003).

I owe a special debt to the late Professor Frederick Rudolph '42, historian of American higher education and author of numerous works concerning Williams College in which the role of fraternities figures prominently. It was Fred who urged me to allow a simple talk on the rise and demise of fraternities to "grow" into what became this book.

To continue the list: Dickinson Debevoise '46, member of the Sterling Committee, the Angevine Committee, and the Standing Committee; Frederic Nathan '43, member of the Sterling Committee and the Angevine Committee; Robert

Geniessee '51, member of the Sterling Committee and the Angevine Committee. (Debevoise, Nathan, and Geniesse later became trustees). E. Wayne Wilkins '41, M.D., president of the Society of Alumni and subsequently trustee during the Sawyer and Chandler administrations; James MacGregor Burns '39, Garfield Club president and later its faculty adviser; Stuart Coan '45; Rhett Austell '48, who was president of the Gargoyle Alumni Association at a crucial moment; the late Andrew Heineman '50, president of the Garfield Club late in its history, member of the Sterling Committee, and a trustee during my administration; Malcolm Kane '54, member of the Garfield Club when it chose to dissolve; the late Hodge Markgraf '52, secretary of the Angevine Committee; Bruce Grinnell '62, a student representative on the Angevine Committee, with whom I have teamed up on numerous occasions for panel discussions and classroom presentations; Robert Durham '62, a student representative on the Angevine Committee; David Phillips '58, chair of the committee that bears his name, whose report revealed patterns of discrimination among fraternities and the existence of secret agreements that forbade the pledging of Jews and blacks; Donald W. (Dee) Gardner, Jr. '57, staff assistant to the Standing Committee and a member of the Committee of 22; Robert Seidman '63, a key member of the discussion group that developed the Grinnell Petition; James Blume '63, who as president of Kappa Alpha and of the Interfraternity Council urged support of the decision of the trustees; President Emeritus Francis C. Oakley, who served as Dean of the Faculty during my administration and succeeded me as president; Professor Benjamin Labaree, Dean of the College from 1963 to 1967; Professor John Hyde '56, who was Dean of Freshmen and then Dean of the College during the Sawyer administration, and whose ancestor, Alexander Hyde, was a member of the student delegation that brought Kappa Alpha to Williams; Jane Dewey and Henry Dewey '48, possessors of correspondence in which Francis Henshaw Dewey of the class of 1840 related his experiences as a Kappa Alpha; Professor Daniel O'Connor, who was Dean of the College during part of my presidency; Professor Neil Grabois, who served in John Sawyer's administration as Dean of the College and then in mine as Dean of the Faculty and as Provost; Professor Stephen Lewis, Jr. '60, who was Provost in both John Sawyer's and my administrations, and later became president of Carleton College; James Briggs '60, who served in a variety of capacities at Williams, including head baseball coach and director of development; Dustin Griffin '65, a long-time trustee of the college; James W. Pilgrim '60; Timothy Blodgett '51; Stephen Franklin '63; Arnold Sher '58; Carl Vogt '58, former president of Williams; Gerry Martin '58, who was treasurer of Phi Gamma Delta; Anthony Smith '57, member of the Committee of 22; Nicholas Wright '57, M.D., also a member of the Committee of 22. I benefited greatly from discussions with current and retired members of the Williams faculty who read earlier drafts of my manuscript, including especially the late Henry Bruton, the late Gordon Winston, Roger Bolton, David Booth, and David Zimmerman. I gratefully acknowledge insights shared by Professors Charles Dew '58 and Will Dudley '89 based upon their experience as chairs of the Committee on Undergraduate Life and information provided by Professor Frank Morgan, faculty adviser to the Dodd Neighborhood.

Materials in the Williams College Archives have been made available to me through the generous and skilled efforts of Sylvia Kennick Brown and Linda Hall. Especially useful were the materials in the fourteen boxes of correspondence and other documents assembled by Standing Committee chairman Ted Banks. Personal papers of John Sawyer that were released in 2012 provided valuable insight and information concerning his interactions with members of the Angevine Committee. Some of the information in this book comes from my unpublished essay, "Reflections on Williams' Presidential Past: Mark Hopkins, Harry Garfield, John E. Sawyer" (2010). In an effort to understand the current structure of residential and social life at Williams, I have benefited from scores of conversations with Williams undergraduates. I also learned much about the neighborhood housing system from conversations with my grandson, Christopher M. Chandler '14 and his thoughtful memorandum based upon conversations with members of the housing office staff, as well as his observations from living in three different neighborhoods and houses, as well as his experience as a first-year resident of Mission Park.

William Boyd, Gordon Davis, and John A. Davis Jr., M.D., members of the class of 1963, contributed importantly to my understanding of how fraternity issues affected the Williams experience of African American students at the end of the fraternity era. Because their fathers graduated from Williams, the Davis cousins have exceptional historical perspectives on these matters.

Over the course of many years I have learned much about the history of fraternities at Amherst College from Charles Longsworth, an Amherst life trustee and former board chair. My understanding of contemporary fraternity issues at Amherst has been significantly informed by conversations with Allen C. Hart, professor of psychology and dean of first year students. I am also grateful to Christina Barber, research specialist at the Amherst College Archives and Special Collections.

I am indebted to the late Carl Westerdahl for his work in securing from the Williams Archives and the collections of the Williamstown Historical Society photographs of fraternities and other Williams buildings that are emblematic of certain eras and themes treated in this study.

As a Senior Fellow at the Francis C. Oakley Center for the Humanities and Social Sciences, I have benefited greatly from the critiques of drafts of this study by two classes of Fellows.

At crucial points along the way, Milton Djuric '80 contributed significantly to the overall argument of the book with his editorial suggestions and research assistance.

I am especially grateful for the interest, encouragement and generous assistance of several administrative officers and staff members of Williams College. These include President Adam Falk; James Kolesar, Vice President for Public Affairs; Robert H. White, Deputy Director of Communications for Alumni Relations and Development; and the book's editor, noted author Hugh Howard.

ENDNOTES

Page 21. *Such is the account...* Personal archives of John M. Hyde, class of 1952, great-grandson of Alexander Hyde, class of 1834, a charter member of Kappa Alpha.

Page 21. *Williams became lost in the shuffle...* "The Establishment of Phi Beta Kappa at Williams," Williams College Archives and Special Collections.

Page 23. *Thereafter its membership...* Frederick Rudolph, *Mark Hopkins and the Log: Williams College, 1836-1872* (Williams College, 1996), p.108.

Page 24. *In 1841, Albert Hopkins...* Journal of the American Education *Society*, vol. XIII, February and May, 1841, pp. 341-51, 461-74).

Page 24. *"the moral darkness of Asia."* Byram Green, a Haystack participant, in Leverett Wilson Spring, *A History of Williams College* (Houghton Mifflin, 1917), p. 79; and Green letter, August 22, 1854, ms. at Williams College Archives and Special Collections.

Page 26. *"house of correction."* Albert Hopkins, "Revivals of Religion in Williams College," (1941), p. 474.

Page 27. *"a new element had found..."* Ibid., p. 471.

Page 27. *"apparently angry conversation."* Ibid., p. 471.

Page 27. *"no room to urge..."* Ibid., p. 472.

Page 28. *"infidel philosophy."* Ibid., p. 342.

Page 28. *"prevailing skepticism..."* Ibid., p. 342.

Page 28. *"The college had come..."* Elon Galusha Salisbury, *In the Days of Mark Hopkins: Story of Williams College* (Phelps, NY: Salisbury Press, 1927), pp. 42-43.

Page 33. *"In serving the religious needs..."* Elizabeth Johnson, "Williams College Christian Associations," http://archives.williams.edu/williamshistory/wca.php.

Page 39. *The Times story carried...* "Williams College Gives Spring Fete," *New York Times*, May 16, 1937, p. 84.

Page 48. *"average scholarship..."* "Fraternities Fail to Face Changed conditions," *Alumni Review*, October 1932, pp. 5-6.

Page 49. *His successor, Tyler Dennett...* James M. Cole '67, "The Dennett Hurricane," Williams College Archives and Special Collections.

Page 53. *Amherst College fared...* See Harold Wade, Jr., *Black Men of Amherst* (Amherst, MA: Amherst College Press, 1976), p.112.

Page 55. *"The answer of the committee..."* Minutes of the Board of Trustees, December 4, 1936.

Page 56. *"and the dogged, overpowering..."* Richard A. Lovell, "Tyler Dennett—New England Frontiersman," *Sketch*, May 1939, p. 30. Williams College Archives and Special Collections.

Page 57. *He described it as...* *Williams Record*, February 23, 1935, p. 1.

Page 57. *"One of the most isolated..."* Russell H. Bostert, ed., *Newhall and Williams College: Selected Papers of a History Teacher at a New England College 1917-1973* (New York: Peter Lang, 1989), pp. 195-196.

Page 59. *"perfect condition..."* *Williams Record*, April 17, 1937, p. 1.

Page 60. *"The Sunday morning chapel..."* President's Report: 1935-1936, pp. 21-22.

Page 65. *To Dennett's suggestion...* Dennett letter of April 20, 1937; Woodbridge reply of April 21, 1937. Williams College Archives and Special Collections.

Page 65. *"He shouts and thunders..."* Richard A. Lovell, "Tyler Dennett—New England Frontiersman," *Sketch*, May 1939.

Page 66. *"the voice of a prophet..."* James M. Cole, "The Dennett Hurricane," p. 44. Williams College Archives and Special Collections.

Page 66. *"Don't compromise yourself..."* *Williams Record*, October 20, 1934, p. 2.

Page 66. *"The college was intended..."* *Williams Record*, November 3, 1934, p.1.

Page 66. *"Today, when the fraternity..."* *Gul* (1939), p. 104.

Page 67. *"Self-made, self reliant, resourceful men..."* *Williams Record*, October 13, 1936, p. 7.

Page 69. *"As to the assumption..."* "Head of Williams Attacks Hopkins," *New York Times*, November 26, 1934, p. 2.

Page 70. *"Becoming increasingly aware of..."* Richard Newhall memorandum, April 20, 1947, Bostert, pp. 201-202.

Page 71. *"Before I entered military..."* Stuart Coan email communication of September 12, 2011.

Page 74. *"The decision of the..."* Faculty Meeting Minutes, December 17, 1951.

Page 75. *Afterwards, President Baxter reiterated...* "Williams Revising Fraternity Plans," *New York Times*, January 23, 1952. p. 29.

Page 88. *"The college's reputation had..."* *Alumni Review*, July, 1961, p. 291.

Page 94. *"I recall vividly..."* Fred Nathan email to author, January 14, 2011.

Page 101. *"total educational experience..."* Angevine Report, p. 5.

Page 102. *"What I'd guessed..."* Sawyer interview with John Walsh, p. 16. Williams College Archives and Special Collections.

Page 103. *"some months ahead of..."* Sawyer to Baxter, June 19, 1962.

Page 113. *"After long consideration the..."* "Statement of the Board of Trustees regarding the Angevine Report," October 6, 1962.

Page 118. *"In short, I am..."* Henry W. Comstock to Talcott Banks, October 23, 1963. Williams College Archives and Special Collections.

Page 119. *"No one has said..."* Jay Angevine to Henry Biggins, November 23, 1962. Williams College Archives and Special Collections.

Page 119. *"If conditions are as..."* Donald Edgar to Talcott Banks, December 19, 1962. Williams College Archives and Special Collections.

Page 120. *John Kifner '63, editor...* *Alumni Review*. February 1963, p. 13.

Page 120. *He expressed doubt that...* Paul Wright to Talcott Banks, December 5, 1962. Williams College Archives and Special Collections.

Page 125. *"fraternities...would be subject..."* Jay Angevine speech, October 6, 1962. Williams College Archives and Special Collections.

Page 230. *"The urgency of pouring..."* John Sawyer to Blake D. Bradford, October 30, 1990, p. 3. Williams College Archives and Special Collections.

Page 132. *By the spring of...* Williams Record, March 22, 1963.

Page 134. *The national Zeta Psi...* Williams Record, April 26, 1963.

Page 134. *"seems recalcitrant."* Williams Record, September 10, 1962.

Page 137. *Wyckoff accused the president...* William O. Wyckoff to John Sawyer, July 13, 1963. Williams College Archives and Special Collections.

Page 140. *The Angevine committee itself...* Angevine Report, p. 10.

Page 140. *"made for a better..."* Fred Rudolph to author, October 8, 2012.

Page 140. *"I learned a lot..."* Gerry Martin email to author, September 28, 2012.

Page 144. *Still, he concluded, the..."* Charles Dew email to author, January 16, 2013.

Page 153. *The trustees of Middlebury...* middlebury.edu; and *New York Times*, April 29, 1994.
Page 000. *The magistrate judge assigned...* Mark D. Bauer, "Small Liberal Arts Colleges, Fraternities, and Antitrust: Rethinking

Hamilton College," in *Catholic University Law Review,* vol. LIII, p. 347.

Page 159. *In a letter to...* John Sawyer to John Redfield, November 22, 1963.

INDEX OF NAMES

A

Agard, Harry, 61
Ahn, Myong-Ku, 90
Alpha Delta Phi, 40, 88, 90, *94*,
   109, 133, 134, 165, 166, 200
Alpha Zeta Alpha, 23, 55, 71,
   81, 165. See also *Phi Gamma
   Delta.*
Alumni Fund, 93, 116, 117,
   125, 137, 138
American Education Society,
   24
American Missionary
   Association, 63
Amherst College, 27, 35, 53,
   73, 81, 123, 157-161, 199,
   206
Angevine Committee, 84, 94,
   97-108, 111, 113, 122, 125,
   126, 128, 132, 134, 137, 140,
   144, *149*, 157, *161*, 203-205
Angevine, Jay, 40, 91, *92*, 93-
   94, 96, 97, 99-108
Anti-Secret Society, 22, 27
Architects Collaborative (TAC),
   130
Armstrong, Samuel Chapman,
   63
Auer, Bernard, 112
Austell, Rhett, 82, 84, 204

B

Banks, Talcott M., 101, 102,
   103, 112=120, 126-128, 133,
   135, 136, 138, 154, 200, 205

Barnett, Vincent, 86
Bascom, John, 31-32, 150
Bates College, 56
Baxter, James Phinney, 25, 53,
   54, 68, *69*, 71-75, 82, 83, 85,
   86-89, 91, 93, 103, 105, 126,
   129, 131, 136, 159, 166, 175,
   177
Beta Theta Pi, 23, 36, 42, 135,
   155, 156, 165, 166, 196
Biggins, Harry, 119
Blume, James, 126, 202
Bolin, Gaius Charles, 63-64
Bowdoin College, 128, 151-152
Brooks, Robert, 68, 128-129
Brown University, 21
Burns, James MacGregor, 65,
   74, *75*, 204

C

Carter, Franklin, 36, *37*, 39-41,
   67, 95, 146, 165, 166, 167
Castle, Ted, 157-158, 159
Chadbourne, Paul Ansel, 23,
   39, 165
Chicago, University of, 62
Chi Psi, 42, 93, 134, 165, 166,
   198, 200
Clark Art Institute, 117, 124,
   190
Coan, Frank, 71
Coan, Stuart, 71, 204
Coffin, William Sloane, 95
Colby College, 151
Cole, James M., 66

213

148, *149*, 150, 151, 159, 160, 162,199-201, 203-205
Sawyer, William H. (Bill), 91
Sawyer, William H., 91, 122
Sayre, Francis, 72, 123
Schuman, Fred, 68
Seidman, Robert, 90, 204
Serkin, Irving, 68
Sewall, Richard, 128
Shainman, Irwin, 68
Shriver Committee, 72, 73, 91, 171
Sigma Phi, 22, 27, 36, 40, 42, 80, 133, 135, 153, 165, 166, 198, 200
Skidmore College, 38
Smith, Anthony, 205
Smith College, 38, 39, 72
Smith, T.C., 57, 65, 69
Social Fraternity of Williams College, 22
Stoddard, Whitney, 114
Stanley, Edward, 92, 95, 183, 201
Sterling Committee, 73, 91, 92, 93, 96, 113, 159, 171, 172, 203-204
Sterling, Dykeman, 73
Street, O. Dickinson, 64

T
Tauber, Kurt, 68
Theta Delta Chi, 36, 132, 134, 165, 166, 196, 197
Thompson, Ben, 130
Thompson, Frederick Ferris, 34, 40, *41*, 42, 95
Thompson, Mary Clark, 34, 40
Thun, Ferdinand, 46, 92, 93, 183
Thun, Peter, 93

Thurston, Ted, 125, 127
Towne, Herbert, 137

U
Union College, 21-22, *24*, 28, 35
Union Theological Seminary, 56
University of Massachusetts-Amherst, 160

V
van Dyke, Henry, 34
Vassar College, 38, 120
Vogt, Carl, 81-82, 140, 205

W
Walsh, John, 101, 102
Watters, Len, 123
Wellesley College, 38
Wesleyan University, 64, 154-156, 199
Westerdahl, Carl, 11, 206
Weston, Karl, 135
White, Stanford, 34, 40
Williams Alumni Action Committee (WAAC), 116, 124, 137, 195-202
Williamstown Historical Society, 11, 12, 206
Williamstown Masonic Lodge, 26-27
Wilson, Woodrow, 43, 48, 103
Woodbridge, Homer, 64-65
World Travel Fellowships, 148
Wright, Paul, 120
Wyckoff, William O., 137
Wynne, Ted, 80-81

About the Author

JOHN W. CHANDLER, the twelfth president of Williams College (1973-1985), is a native of North Carolina. After graduating from Wake Forest College with *magna cum laude* and Phi Beta Kappa honors, he received his Ph.D. degree from Duke University in philosophy of religion. After teaching briefly in the department of philosophy at Wake Forest, he joined the department of religion at Williams in 1955 as an assistant professor. During the next decade, he achieved tenure, became chair of his department, established a major in religion, and chaired the ad hoc committee whose proposals resulted in a new curriculum that included Winter Study. In 1965 President Sawyer established the office of dean of the faculty and named Chandler to the post. Chandler left Williams to become president of Hamilton College in 1968. He returned to Williams as president in 1973. Upon retiring in 1985, he became president of the Association of American Colleges and Universities (1985-1990). Among the various boards of trustees on which he served was that of Duke University, where he became chair. From 1990 to 2001, he assisted more than forty colleges and universities with presidential searches.

$25.00
ISBN 978-0-915081-07-3
52500>

9 780915 081073